FAMOUS FRENCH COOKERY

By
Hyla O'Connor

Fawcett Publications, Inc.
67 West 44th Street
New York, N.Y. 10019

CONTENTS

LARRY EISINGER: *Editor-in-Chief*

GEORGE TILTON: *Executive Editor*

SILVIO LEMBO: *Creative Director* • HAROLD E. PRICE: *Associate Director*

ELLENE SAUNDERS: *Editor*

PAMELA RIDDLE: *Editorial Assistant*

HERBERT JONAS: *Layout*   ALLEN WILSON: *Layout*

ELAINE E. SAPOFF: *Production Editor*   ALAINE TROW: *Production Assistant*

Editorial Staff: JOE PIAZZA, RAY GILL,
DAN BLUE, FRANK BOWERS, AMY MORRIS

Art Staff: MIKE GAYNOR, ALEX SANTIAGO, JOHN SELVAGGIO,
JOHN CERVASIO, JACK LA CERRA, JOSEPH MAYA

Ralph Owen, Decorative Art

Printed in U.S.A. by
FAWCETT-HAYNES PRINTING CORPORATION
Rockville, Maryland

INTRODUCTION

Mention French food and French cooking and everyone immediately thinks of the Grande Cuisine. But what of French home cooking? Like her American counterpart, the French housewife has three meals to cook each day, and pressed duck or flaming crêpes are not a part of her family's daily fare. She cooks with ingredients that are at hand, stewing, simmering and flavoring much the same as any busy American wife and mother.

When she yearns for fancy food, the French woman dines out, just as we are wont to do here in America. Food served in a top flight French or American restaurant is much more elegant because all the cooking is not done by just one person. There are many chefs, each handling a specific job—meats, sauces, vegetables, etc.—as well as the grand master chef, who oversees the whole operation and is the soul of a really good restaurant. For at-home parties, the French hostess orders pâté en croûte or a fancy main dish from a store in the neighborhood that specializes in select cooked meat dishes. Then she completes her meal with a selection of wondrous desserts from the local bakery.

Americans tend to think of French food as being invariably covered with rich cream sauces or simmered in wine and blazing in cognac. But again, just as a cook in Georgia prepares Southern Fried Chicken or a Maine housewife makes New England Chowder, the French woman turns out the various regional specialties which her country offers. These dishes evolve, as they do in America, because of the food and produce raised in the area. Dairying, for example, is a major industry in Normandy and the dishes of the region tend to be rich with butter and cream. Since apples are abundant, many of the dishes are cooked with cider or applejack. Fish dishes are popular all over France because the country is surrounded on three sides by water and many rivers flow through it. Wine is as common for a French woman to cook with as water is for us, because wine is produced in almost every part of the country. It is used as a flavoring to add to the taste of a dish, much as we use onions or other spices.

Thanks to the gourmet corner in most supermarkets, you will be able to find the items you need to prepare the recipes in this book. Expensive truffles and pâtés are used here for flavoring and are fun to use for special occasions regardless of cost.

Shallots, those tangy members of the onion family, are being carried by many supermarkets. If you see them, buy a few, for they keep well and you can use them on your next French cooking spree.

You probably will not need any special equipment for French cooking. A set of good knives is, of course, a must, and learning the art of using a French knife can make cutting chores easier. A set of heavy pots and pans will fill the bill for the long, slow cooking of stews and sauces. The only thing to remember is to use either an enamel or stainless steel pot when cooking with white wine, to prevent the sauce from turning dark. You may want an omelet or crêpe pan, and if you're planning on soufflés, a straight-sided soufflé dish is necessary.

Other basics include wooden spoons for stirring, rubber scrapers for getting out the last drop, and wire whisks for beating and making smooth, creamy sauces. Beating egg whites can be done with a whisk if you have a good right arm, but a rotary beater works just as well.

Now that you have a little background and knowledge of the tools you'll need, it's time to start exploring the delectable world of French cooking.

Bread, Cheese, & Wine

Served with all meals and a must with cheese and wine, bread is truly the staff of life for the French people. It is not uncommon for them to make as many as three daily trips to the baker. The first purchase is made early in the morning. French breakfasts or "petits dejeuners" are much lighter than ours, consisting of an assortment of rolls (croissants and brioches) and French bread served with café au lait, a delicious blend of half hot coffee and half hot milk. The bread is always freshly baked and warm—a delightful breakfast. If lunch is eaten at home, bread is bought again, and another trip to the "boulangerie" is a must before dinner.

French housewives rarely do their own bread baking, preferring the baker's inimitable crusty loaves. Even rural areas are supplied by bakery trucks from the town, ensuring each French family of its "petit pain". A common sight in French towns is French children improvising walking sticks and bats from loaves of bread intended for the family table. The long loaves are seen peeping out of housewives' shopping bags or dangling from their bicycle baskets.

Unfortunately, the bread produced in France could never really be duplicated here, for they use a different type of flour, different ovens, and different baking techniques. However, we are including recipes for bread, croissants, and for brioches which will be great fun to try. Serve them at a leisurely Sunday brunch along with a hearty platter of bacon and eggs, or try them the French way with butter and café au lait.

In France, the favorite part of a meal, or in many cases the whole meal, is an assortment of cheeses served with crusty French bread and a glass of wine. This is a custom which can well be adapted to American dining, if not for every day, certainly for special occasions or light meals.

You are undoubtedly familiar with the kinds of domestic cheese made in America. We have American cheddar, liederkranz, Swiss, cream, cottage, Monterey Jack and a few specialty cheeses. Many of these are used for sandwiches, salads and dips, but they also take kindly to the French treatment with bread and wine.

The marriage of cheese and wine is one of the world's most enduring. Dry red wine is best with most cheeses. The tangier the cheese, the more full-bodied the wine should be. Dry white wine is excellent with goat cheeses and champagne is wonderful with all cheeses.

French cheeses should be removed from the refrigerator one to two hours before serving because they are best enjoyed at room temperature. Round cheeses, such as Brie, Camembert or Port Salut should always be cut from the center out so that everyone can enjoy the tasty center.

If you are not familiar with French cheeses, here is an introductory assortment. After you have tried these, branch out and try other kinds, not only from France, but from many other parts of the world as well—there are as many as 2000 different varieties!

Wine is a traditional part of the French diet, and any French meal is considered incomplete without a good wine to complement the food. This does not mean that a great vintage wine is served with every meal, but there is always at least an inexpensive vin ordinaire. Even in France, the great wines are reserved for the great occasions.

There are several schools of thought concerning the selection of wines. Dyed-in-the-wool purists insist that there is no wine like the native French product, while others will defend the domestic varieties from California and New York. The finest vineyards in California are located in the San Francisco Bay region and produce many good wines, both red and white. As with French wines, there are many great California wines. A label with the name of the grape or the name of the vintner is a good guide to choosing a good wine. There are also excellent inexpensive wines produced in California. New York State has several outstanding wine companies. The grapes, which are strictly American, produce an entirely different kind of wine. Taste and experiment, to find the ones that agree with your palate.

Any wine expert will tell you that the average person should drink the wine that tastes the best to him, without regard for things like vintage years and labels. Start your wine education by trying wines that appeal to your pocketbook and taste. Judge wine, as a professional does, by appearance, aroma or bouquet, and taste. First, hold the glass by the stem, raise it to the light and check the color and clarity. All wines should be crystal clear. Any cloudiness means that the wine is sick and may not be good. Swirl the wine gently in the glass to release the bouquet, and then take a hearty sniff. You can judge the wine

Golden brown and buttery, flaky Brioche can be a real treat when served piping hot for breakfast with a steaming cup of strong coffee with hot milk.

Fleischman's Yeast

by the pleasant aroma. Eventually, you will be able to distinguish many wines by the aroma alone. Finally, you are ready to sip the wine. For full enjoyment, hold the wine in your mouth for a moment and roll it around the tongue before swallowing it.

The wines of the world are divided into two general categories, table wines and dessert or appetizer wines. The differences between the two are the alcoholic content and the relative dryness. The table wines generally have an alcoholic content of about 12 per cent. As a rule, they are dry wines and are served with the main part of the meal. Appetizer wines, such as sherry and Dubonnet, are of higher alcoholic content and served before or between meals. Dessert wines are generally served after the main part of the meal, with dessert. Here the alcoholic content is about 20 per cent. Falling in between are the rosés and champagne which can be served before, during and after meals.

Wine is a living thing and should be treated as such. French wines have a life cycle of youth, maturity, old age and death. This means that wines keep on working and growing right up to the time they are consumed. Some wines taste best when they are young and others have to mature for several years before they reach a peak of perfection. Good wines should be stored on their sides, to keep the cork moist, and kept in a dark, well-ventilated place at a temperature of around 50°F. They should never be shaken.

There is much discussion about wine glasses. If you do not have a different glass for each kind of wine, do not despair. An all-purpose wine glass made from clear glass with a stem and a capacity of eight to nine ounces, will serve every need. When serving wine, fill the glass half full (less if serving sweet wine) to allow room in the top for the aroma to gather, so that it can be inhaled as well as drunk. Champagne is no longer served in flat champagne glasses, for this is a quick way to lose all the bubbles; use your all-purpose tulip-shaped glass for champagne also.

Red wines are served at room temperature. This does not mean that they should be warmed, but should always be brought out of storage about four hours before being served. The cork should be removed about one-half hour to an hour before serving to allow the wine time to breathe. White wines, rosés and champagnes are always served chilled. They can be refrigerated two to four hours before serving. They should never be placed in the freezer, for if they are too cold, they lose much of their taste.

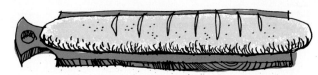

Appetizer or apéritif wines are sweetened, fortified and flavored before-dinner wines. Some of the most popular in the United States are Dubonnet, either red or white, Byrrh, vermouth, and sherry. In France, the before-dinner drinking is limited to one, because the dinner is going to have wine with it and they do not like to linger and ruin their appetites before beginning the feast. An apéritif is served to stimulate the palate for the food to come. The prolonged American cocktail hour is no time to serve your best wine. Reserve it for true wine lovers.

As a rule of thumb, red wines are used for red meats and game. Light-bodied red wines from the Bordeaux area complement turkey, veal and lamb. They also go well with beef and lamb stews, bouillabaisse, hamburgers, steaks and patés. Rich, full-bodied red wines from Burgundy go with richer meats such as duck, goose, kidneys, games and meats marinated in red wine. Red wines are also excellent with cheeses, although some mild flavored cheeses may call for a white wine.

White wines can be either dry or sweet, depending upon personal preference. Sweet white wines, such as sauternes, make excellent dessert wines and go well with a very rich foie gras or paté, but some people like them with the entire dinner. Serve dry white wines with fish and shellfish, egg dishes, poultry and very light veal dishes. Although white wines are generally used with white meats, if the fish or poultry has been prepared with a red wine, one should drink a red wine with it to complement the taste of the dish.

Rosé wines can be served with anything and can go right through a whole dinner as the basic wine.

Champagnes can be served and enjoyed with any kind of food at any time. Start with a Brut (dry) champagne with the appetizer, continue with dry champagne with the main course, and finish off with a sweet champagne with dessert and coffee. However, even in France, champagne is something special and reserved for festive occasions.

Dessert wines are sweet wines to complement the ending of a meal. They can be Madeira, sauterne, cream sherry or not-too-dry champagne. Port becomes an after-dessert drink because it is very rich and heavy, pleasant to sip with nuts or candies.

PETITS BRIOCHES

½ cup milk
½ cup butter or margarine
⅓ cup sugar
1 teaspoon salt
¼ cup warm water (105-115°F.)
1 package or cake yeast, active dry or compressed
3 whole eggs
1 egg yolk
3½ cups unsifted flour
1 egg white
1 tablespoon sugar

1. Scald milk and cool to lukewarm.
2. Cream butter or margarine in large mixing bowl. Gradually add sugar and salt and cream until light and fluffy.
3. Measure water into a small warm bowl. Sprinkle or crumble in yeast and stir until dissolved.
4. Add lukewarm milk, dissolved yeast, eggs, egg yolk and flour to creamed butter mixture. With a wooden spoon beat vigorously for 2 minutes.
5. Cover bowl and let rise in a warm place, free from draft, until more than doubled in bulk (about 2 hours).
6. Stir down and beat vigorously for 2 minutes. Cover tightly with aluminum foil and refrigerate overnight.
7. In the morning beat down the dough. Turn soft dough out on a lightly floured board. Divide into 2 pieces, one about ¾ of the dough and the other about ¼ of the dough.
8. Cut large piece into 24 equal small pieces. Form into smooth balls. Place balls in well greased medium-sized muffin pans. Cut smaller piece into 24 equal pieces. Form into smooth balls.
9. Make a deep indentation in center of each large ball. Dampen slightly with cold water. Press a small ball into each indentation.
10. Let rise in a warm place, free from draft, until doubled in bulk, about 50 minutes.
11. Heat oven to 375°F.
12. Beat together 1 egg white and 1 tablespoon sugar.
13. Brush top of each brioche lightly with beaten egg.
14. Bake 15 to 20 minutes, or until lightly browned and baked.
15. Turn out of pans immediately to cool.
16. Makes 2 dozen brioches.

RAPID MIX FRENCH BREAD

3 to 3½ cups unsifted flour, divided
4 teaspoons sugar
1½ teaspoons salt
1 package active dry yeast
2 tablespoons soft margarine
1¼ cups very hot tap water
Corn meal
1 egg white, slightly beaten
1 tablespoon water

1. In a large bowl throughly mix 1 cup flour, sugar, salt and active dry yeast. Add soft margarine.
2. Gradually add very hot tap water to dry ingredients and beat 2 minutes at medium speed of electric mixer, scraping bowl occasionally. Add 1 cup flour, or enough to make a thick batter. Beat at high speed for 2 minutes, scraping bowl occasionally. Stir in enough additional flour to make a soft dough.
3. Cover bowl tightly with plastic wrap or aluminum foil and let stand 45 minutes.
4. Stir down dough and turn out onto a heavily floured board. With floured hands mold into an oblong, 15 inches long. Taper ends. Sprinkle a baking sheet with corn meal. Carefully place dough on baking sheet. Cover and let rise in a warm place, free from draft, until doubled in bulk, about 40 minutes.
5. Heat oven to 400°F.
6. With a sharp knife, make 5 diagonal cuts on top of leaf. Bake 25 minutes. Brush loaf with combined beaten egg white and cold water. Return to oven and bake 15 minutes longer, or until done.
7. Remove from baking sheet and cool on wire rack.
8. Makes 1 large loaf.

¾ cup butter or margarine
3 cups unsifted flour, divided
¾ cup milk
¼ cup warm water (105-115°F.)
1 package or cake yeast, active dry or compressed
3 tablespoons sugar
1 teaspoon salt
1 egg, beaten
1 egg
1 tablespoon milk
Sugar

1. Work butter or margarine into ¼ cup unsifted flour until mixture is smooth paste. Place between two sheets of waxed paper and roll into a 10- by 4-inch rectangle. Chill for 1 hour.
2. When margarine mixture is chilled, prepare dough. Scald milk and cool to lukewarm.
3. Measure warm water into a large warm bowl. Sprinkle or crumble in yeast and stir until dissolved. Stir in 3 tablespoons sugar, salt, beaten egg and 1 cup flour. Beat until smooth. Stir in remaining flour until completely blended.
4. Turn dough out onto a well floured board. Roll out into a 12-inch square. Carefully peel waxed paper away from chilled butter or margarine slab. Place slab over center third of dough. Fold an outside third of dough over the center third then cover with remaining third of dough. Give dough a quarter turn. Roll out into a 12-inch square. Fold in thirds as before. Turn dough, roll and fold 3 more times. Wrap in waxed paper and chill for 2 hours.
5. Divide chilled dough in thirds. Shape one third at a time, refrigerating the remainder. Roll one third out on a lightly floured board into a circle 12 inches in diameter. Cut into 8 pie-shaped wedges or pieces. Beat together 1 egg and 1 tablespoon milk, Brush point of each piece with egg mixture. Roll each piece up tightly, beginning at wide end. Seal points. Place on a greased baking sheet with points underneath. Curve to form crescents. Brush with egg mixture and sprinkle with sugar. Repeat with remaining dough.
6. Let rise in a warm place, free from draft, until light, about 30 minutes.
7. Heat oven to 375°F.
8. Bake about 12 minutes or until lightly browned and done.
9. Makes 24 croissants.

Note: To freeze croissants, wrap tightly in aluminum foil and place in freezer. To thaw, heat in unopened foil wrapping in hot oven (400°F.) 15 to 20 minutes, or until warm.

PICTURED FRENCH CHEESES

1. **Valençay** (vah-lahn-say) A pyramid shaped goat cheese. The crust is usually scraped before it is eaten. Goat cheese comes in many varieties, sizes and shapes. All have a special flavor and are highly appreciated by cheese fanciers.

2. **Caprice des Dieux** (kah-prees-day-dyoo) A mild, soft, buttery cheese shaped in an oval. The edge of the crust is usually cut away. The rest of the crust may or may not be eaten as desired.

3. **Roquefort** (rowk-for) A genuine Roquefort is aged in the famous natural caves in the town for which it is named. It is made exclusively from ewes' milk and is marked with green streaks which help impart the cheese's tangy flavor.

4. **Grape or Tomme au Marc** (tum-oh-mark) An interesting and tasty cheese the crust of which is made with grape pulp (marc) that remains after grapes are pressed for wine. It has a delicate distinctive flavor and creamy texture. The crust is generally not eaten.

5. **Pont L'Eveque** (Pohn-l'eh-vek) A soft, yellow, paste cheese with thousands of tiny holes. It has a rich hearty flavor. The crust may or may not be eaten. Usually the buttery crust is scraped and the edges cut before eating.

6. **Port de Salut** (pohr-duh-saloo) This yellow, smooth, buttery cheese with its mellow flavor was originated by Trappist monks in Brittany over 150 years ago. It is a pasteurized cheese sold in wedges and small and large wheels. Similar cheeses are St. Paulin and Bonbel.

7. **Brie** (bree) A soft, creamy, pale yellow cheese with a buttery crust which may be eaten. It is often referred to as the "prince of cheeses".

8. **Roblochon** (roh-bluh-shun) This buttery cheese is produced high in the Alps and seems to retain a good deal of the aroma of the mountain air. The crust is not eaten.

9. **Carré de l'Este** (kah-reh-duh l'est) This is a soft buttery cheese with a delicately sharp flavor. The crust may or may not be eaten. The unusual flavor of this cheese is attributed to the qualities of the chalky soils where the cows graze.

10. **Camembert** (kah-mem-behr) A soft cheese, creamy in texture, with a delicately pungent flavor. The buttery crust is edible. Camembert ripens slowly and is at its best when yellow in color and has the same consistency throughout.

11. **Bonbel** (bone-bell) Similar in taste to the Port de Salut.

12. **Camembert** An individual portion is shown.

Appetizers and Soups

In France most meals begin with a variety of appetizers or a soup, just as they end with a variety of cheeses and fresh fruit. Country restaurants serve a first course consisting of an astonishing array of cold vegetables marinated to perfection, a whole board loaded with sausages and smoked meats, and always the pâté of the restaurant or the area, called a Pâté Maison.

For a grand feast at home, there is an overwhelming variety of appetizers. If the main part of the meal is light, the housewife rounds out the meal with several appetizers. However, most days she has only one or two very simple dishes to start a meal.

In this country, our food and eating habits are different. We usually serve a variety of these foods only when we are entertaining. Many would make wonderful hors d'oeuvres for your next party, or you may like to try one or two of them as a first course, served in the French manner with French bread and a bottle of wine.

CHICKEN LIVER PÂTÉ

½ envelope (1½ teaspoons) unflavored gelatine
½ cup bouillon or consommé
Pimiento
Capers
Truffles or ripe olives
1 pound chicken livers
½ teaspoon Ac'cent
6 tablespoons butter or margarine, divided
2 tablespoons minced onion
½ teaspoon salt
1 teaspoon dry mustard
¼ teaspoon cloves
⅛ teaspoon nutmeg
2 tablespoons brandy

1. Sprinkle gelatine over bouillon in a small saucepan to soften. Place over low heat, stirring constantly, until gelatine is dissolved. Pour a thin layer of the bouillon mixture in bottom of an 8- by 4- by 2½-inch loaf pan. Let thicken slightly. Press a design of pimiento, capers and truffles into thickened bouillon. Pour remaining bouillon mixture carefully over design and chill while preparing pâté mixture.
2. Sprinkle chicken livers with Ac'cent. Melt 2 tablespoons of the butter in a skillet. Sauté chicken livers and onion in the butter for 6 or 7 minutes. Remove from heat.
3. Scrape chicken and onions into blender container. Add salt, dry mustard, cloves and nutmeg. Turn on blender and blend until smooth. Add remaining 4 tablespoons butter and brandy. Blend until smooth.
4. Turn mixture into prepared loaf pan. Chill.
5. To unmold, quickly dip pan in hot water up to top. Loosen with a sharp knife. Invert on a serving platter.
6. Makes 24 servings.

Shown: Chicken Liver Pâté, Lobster Barquettes, Almond Mushrooms, Stuffed Tomatoes, Deviled Eggs, Crabmeat Quiche, Vegetables Vinaigrette.

Ac'cent

LOBSTER BARQUETTES

1 package (10 ounces) pie crust mix
1 tablespoon butter
1 can (5 ounces) lobster, finely chopped
1 tablespoon chopped onion
1 tablespoon snipped parsley
2 tablespoons brandy
½ teaspoon Ac'cent
2 teaspoons lemon juice
⅓ cup warm light cream
1 egg yolk
Grated Parmesan cheese
Buttered bread crumbs

1. Heat oven to 375°F.
2. Prepare pie crust mix according to package directions. Roll dough out on a lightly floured board to ⅛-inch thickness. Invert 3-inch barquette molds on dough. With a sharp knife cut ⅓ inch out from edge of each mold. Fit piece of cut out pastry into each mold; press down to bottom and sides with finger tips. Trim excess pastry around rim of mold. Prick bottom all over with a fork. Fit a small piece of foil in each barquette. Fill shells with rice or beans. Bake 10 minutes. Remove from oven and remove foil with rice or beans. Return to oven and bake until bottom is lightly browned. Cool shells and remove carefully from molds.
3. Melt butter in a skillet. Add lobster, onion and parsley. Cook gently until onion is tender but not browned.
4. Remove from heat and stir in brandy. Sprinkle with Ac'cent and lemon juice. Combine warm cream and egg yolk. Stir into skillet. Spoon mixture into baked barquettes. Sprinkle with Parmesan cheese and bread crumbs.
5. Heat broiling compartment of range. Put barquettes on broiler pan and broil, about 5 inches from source of heat, until lightly browned.
6. Makes about 16 barquettes.

ALMOND MUSHROOMS

1 pound large mushrooms, about 1½ dozen
  Ac'cent
⅓ cup dry bread crumbs
2 teaspoons lemon juice
⅛ teaspoon rosemary
⅛ teaspoon marjoram
¼ teaspoon salt
¼ cup finely chopped almonds
1 tablespoon capers, optional
3 tablespoons butter
3 tablespoons finely snipped parsley

1. Heat oven to 350°F.
2. Wash mushrooms. Remove stems and reserve. Pat mushroom caps dry with paper toweling. Sprinkle inside of mushroom caps with Ac'cent.
3. Chop mushroom stems very fine. Combine with bread crumbs, lemon juice, rosemary, marjoram, salt, almonds and capers. Spoon mixture into mushroom caps. Place in a greased shallow baking pan. Dot each mushroom with butter.
4. Bake 20 to 25 minutes.
5. Sprinkle with chopped parsley and serve immediately.
6. Makes 1½ dozen mushrooms.

STUFFED TOMATOES

1 pint cherry tomatoes
1 can (7 ounces) tuna fish
¼ teaspoon salt
½ teaspoon curry powder
2½ tablespoons mayonnaise
2 teaspoons lemon juice
2 teaspoons onion powder
  Parsley

1. Rinse tomatoes with cold water and pat dry with paper toweling. With a sharp knife, cut a circle in top of each tomato and remove about half the pulp. Invert tomatoes and allow to drain.
2. Drain tuna and break in small pieces. Add remaining ingredients and toss until well blended.
3. Stuff tomatoes with tuna mixture. Refrigerate until serving time.
4. Garnish with parsley.
5. Makes enough stuffing for 20 to 25 tomatoes.

DEVILED EGGS

6 hard-cooked eggs
¼ cup mayonnaise
1 teaspoon vinegar
½ teaspoon Worcestershire sauce
¼ teaspoon dry mustard
  Rolled anchovies
  Pimiento

1. Peel eggs and carefully cut in halves lengthwise. Remove egg yolks, being careful not to break egg whites.
2. Mash egg yolks with a fork. Mix with mayonnaise, vinegar, Worcestershire sauce and dry mustard.
3. Spoon mixture into egg white halves. Refrigerate until ready to serve.
4. Garnish tops of eggs with rolled anchovies or pimiento.
5. Makes 12 halves.

CRABMEAT QUICHE

1 8-inch unbaked pie shell
2 eggs
1 cup light cream
1 teaspoon Ac'cent
¾ teaspoon salt
¹⁄₁₆ teaspoon cayenne pepper
3 ounces Swiss cheese, grated
3 ounces Gruyere cheese, grated
1 tablespoon flour
1 can (6½ ounces) crabmeat, flaked

1. Heat oven to 450°F.
2. Prick bottom and sides of pie shell with a fork. Bake until delicately brown, about 10 minutes.
3. Beat together eggs, cream, Ac'cent, salt and cayenne. Combine grated cheese, flour and crabmeat. Sprinkle evenly over bottom of pie shell. Pour cream mixture over top.
4. Lower oven heat to 325°F. Bake quiche 45 minutes to 1 hour, or until tip of knife inserted in center comes out clean.
5. Cut in small wedges for appetizers or large pieces for a luncheon dish.
6. Makes 16 small servings.

A Veal and Ham Mousse is easy to prepare and can be made well in advance. Served with crackers or bread it can accompany cocktails with elegance.

National Biscuit Co.

ONION QUICHE

1 9-inch unbaked pie shell
3 eggs
½ cup milk
½ cup light cream
¾ teaspoon salt
½ teaspoon Tabasco
⅛ teaspoon nutmeg
¼ pound Swiss cheese, grated
¼ pound Gruyére cheese, grated
1 tablespoon flour
1 large onion, cut into quarters and thinly sliced

1. Heat oven to 450°F.
2. Prick pie shell all over with a fork. Bake 5 to 10 minutes or until delicately brown. Remove pie shell and reduce oven heat to 325°F.
3. Beat together eggs, milk, cream, salt, Tabasco and nutmeg. Combine grated cheese and flour. Sprinkle evenly in pie shell. Pour in cream mixture. Top with onion slices.
4. Bake 45 minutes or until point of knife inserted in center of pie comes out clean.
5. Makes 16 appetizers or 6 luncheon servings.

VEGETABLES VINAIGRETTE

Cooked vegetables, marinated in some kind of French dressing are always a part of hors d'oeuvres or appetizer service in France. Here are a few that you may like to try.

White Beans: Sprinkle ½ teaspoon Ac'cent over 3 cups cooked white beans. Add 1 chopped onion and 2 tablespoons snipped parsely to beans. Add 1 cut clove of garlic and ½ cup French dressing. Toss lightly and chill thoroughly. Remove garlic before serving.

Cucumbers: Peel and cut 3 cucumbers into very thin slices. Use a vegetable peeler for paper-thin slices. Combine ½ cup vinegar with 2 tablespoons sugar and 2 tablespoons water. Pour over cucumbers. Add 1 cut clove garlic and sprinkle with chopped dill. Chill thoroughly. Remove garlic before serving.

Artichoke Hearts: Drain 2 cans (1 pound each) artichoke hearts. Sprinkle with 1 teaspoon Ac'cent. Add ½ cup French dressing and 2 tablespoons lemon juice. Sprinkle with diced pimiento and capers. Toss lightly and marinate in refrigerator.

French Onion Soup is almost as popular as the Eiffel Tower. Hearty beef stock, rich with onions, makes a whole meal served with French bread.

Salton Inc.

MUSHROOMS À LA GRÈCQUE

½ pound small mushrooms
Juice of ½ lemon
½ teaspoon salt
¼ teaspoon freshly ground black pepper
1 tablespoon olive oil
1 teaspoon prepared mustard
1 tablespoon chopped parsley

1. Wash and trim mushrooms. Leave whole. Place in a small saucepan with lemon juice, salt, pepper and oil. Cover. Cook for 10 minutes. Let stand in juice until cool.
2. Chill in refrigerator in liquid until cold.
3. Place mushrooms in a serving dish. Blend mustard and marinade well and pour over mushrooms. Sprinkle with parsley.
4. Makes 4 servings.

VEAL AND HAM MOUSSE

1 envelope unflavored gelatine
¼ cup cold water
½ cup boiling water
1 can (10½ ounces) condensed beef consomme
½ cup mayonnaise
¾ teaspoon salt
¼ teaspoon nutmeg
1 tablespoon grated lemon peel
1 tablespoon minced onion
½ cup finely minced celery
2½ cups ground cooked veal
1 cup ground cooked ham
½ cup onion cracker crumbs, (approximately 10 crackers, finely rolled)
1 cup heavy cream, whipped

1. Soften gelatine in cold water. Add the boiling water and stir until the gelatine is dissolved. Add consomme.
2. Measure out ¾ cup of the consomme mixture. Pour into a lightly oiled 9-inch loaf pan. Chill until just set.
3. In a large bowl combine mayonnaise, salt, nutmeg, lemon peel, onion and celery. Stir in remaining consomme mixture. Fold in veal, ham and crumbs. Fold in whipped cream.
4. Pour mixture over set aspic in bottom of loaf pan. Chill 5 to 6 hours or overnight in the refrigerator.
5. Unmold on a large serving platter. Garnish top with pasteurized processed cheese spread from a pressure can, if desired.
6. Makes 10 to 12 first course servings.

ESCARGOTS BOURGUIGNONNE

1 can (4 ounces) escargots (French snails)
Red wine
Bay leaf
1 clove garlic, crushed
6 peppercorns
1 package snail seasoning
4 tablespoons sweet butter, softened

1. Heat oven to 425°F.
2. Drain escargots and discard liquid. Place in a bowl. Cover with red wine. Add bay leaf, garlic and peppercorns. Place in refrigerator and let stand at least 24 hours. Toss occasionally.
3. Prepare snail seasoning according to package directions using 4 tablespoons of butter instead of 6 tablespoons called for on package. Drain escargots.
4. Put a dollop of seasoned butter on one end of each escargot; insert in shell, butter side down. Place an additional small dollop of seasoned butter on top of each escargot.
5. Place shells in escargots dish. If you do not have a dish, half fill a baking pan with heavy coarse salt. Stand shells in salt so that they will not tip over during baking.
6. Bake 10 to 15 minutes, or until butter is bubbly.
7. Makes 18 to 24 escargots.

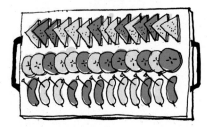

MOUSSE AU ROQUEFORT

6 egg yolks
6 tablespoons cream
1½ envelopes unflavored gelatine
¼ cup cold water
¾ pound Roquefort cheese
1½ cups heavy cream, whipped
3 egg whites, stiffly beaten
Watercress

1. In the top part of a double boiler beat the egg yolks with 6 tablespoons cream. Set over hot water and beat the mixture until it has thickened slightly and is creamy.
2. Soften gelatine in cold water. Add to egg yolk mixture and stir until gelatine is completely dissolved. Remove from heat.
3. Force Roquefort cheese through a sieve, add to egg yolk mixture, stirring until well blended.
4. Cool mixture. Fold in whipped cream. Fold in stiffly beaten egg whites.
5. Pour the mousse into an oiled mold. Chill for 2 hours or until mixture is firm.
6. Unmold mousse on a chilled serving plate and garnish with watercress. Serve with rounds of toast.

BEEF STOCK

2½ pounds soup meat
3 tablespoons butter or margarine
1½ pounds marrow bones, sawed in small pieces
3 quarts cold water
1 tablespoon salt
2 onions, each stuck with 2 cloves
3 or 4 carrots
2 stalks celery
3 sprigs parsley
1 bay leaf
2 leeks, cleaned thoroughly
Sprig of thyme or pinch of dried thyme
2 egg whites, optional

1. Cut soup meat in chunks. Melt butter in heavy, deep kettle. Add meat and bones and brown quickly, stirring occasionally.
2. Add cold water. Bring to a boil and boil briskly a few minutes, then skim the top off the liquid. Reduce heat to low, cover and simmer about 3 hours.
3. Skim off the foam that forms on top of the soup from time to time during cooking process.
4. After 1 hour of cooking add salt, onions, carrots, celery, parsley, bay leaf, leeks, and thyme. Continue simmering.
5. Strain the hot soup through cheese cloth into a bowl. Let stand 5 minutes and skim fat off surface with a spoon. Wrap paper towel around an ice cube and use to collect the small particles of fat that float on the surface.
6. If you are not going to use the stock immediately, chill in the refrigerator and skim off fat easily when it has all risen to the top and solidified.
7. If you wish to clarify the broth, combine it with 2 egg whites, lightly beaten. Allow to come to a boil and boil for 2 minutes. Strain through 2 layers of cheese cloth.
8. The beef stock may be frozen and used in recipes calling for stock or bouillon.
9. It may be served as soup with the addition of vegetables, tiny pastas etc.
10. Makes 2½ to 3 quarts stock.

ONION SOUP

1½ pounds dry onions
4 tablespoons butter
2 tablespoons salad oil
1 teaspoon salt
Pinch of sugar
2 tablespoons flour
2 quarts canned beef bouillon
½ cup dry white wine or dry white vermouth
Bread
Swiss or Parmesan cheese, grated

1. Peel and cut onions in very thin slices. Melt butter and oil in a large saucepan or a heavy Dutch oven. Add onions and simmer over low heat about 15 minutes.
2. Sprinkle salt and sugar over onions. Raise heat to moderate and cook about 30 minutes, stirring occasionally, until onions are tender and have turned an even golden brown.
3. Sprinkle flour over top of onions and stir and cook for 2 minutes.
4. Stir in beef bouillon and wine. Taste and add salt and pepper if necessary. Simmer for 30 to 40 minutes.
5. Serve piping hot with slices of plain or toasted French bread and grated Swiss or Parmesan cheese.
6. Makes 6 to 8 servings.

CONSOMMÉ

2½ pounds lean stew beef
2 tablespoons butter
1½ pounds marrow bone
1½ pounds veal knuckle
3½ quarts water
1 pound chicken wings and backs
2 onions stuck with 4 cloves
4 carrots, sliced
3 whole stalks celery, with leaves
3 to 4 leeks, cleaned and sliced
1½ tablespoons salt
3 sprigs parsley
2 sprigs thyme or a pinch of dried thyme
1 clove garlic
1 bay leaf
6 peppercorns
2 egg whites

1. Cut 1½ pounds of the beef in 1-inch cubes. Leave remainder in 1 piece.
2. Melt butter in a large heavy soup kettle. Add beef cubes and brown quickly on all sides.
3. Add whole piece of meat, marrow bone, veal knuckle and water. Bring to a boil and allow to boil a few minutes. Skim off foam from top.
4. Lower heat, cover and simmer about 1 hour.
5. Add chicken wings and backs, onions, carrots, celery, leeks, salt, parsley, thyme, garlic, bay leaf and peppercorns. Cover and simmer about 4 hours. Skim occasionally.
6. Strain the hot soup through cheese cloth into a bowl. Let stand 5 minutes and skim fat off surface with a spoon. Wrap paper towel around an ice cube and use to collect the small particles of fat that float around on the surface.
7. You may chill the consommé quickly, then skim off all the fat that has risen to the surface and solidified.
8. Combine the stock with 2 beaten egg whites. Bring to a boil and boil for 2 minutes. Strain through 2 layers of cheese cloth.
9. Serve hot or cold. Taste for seasonings.
10. Makes about 3 quarts.

Variations

Add a small amount of cooked rice or cooked pastas in fancy shapes. . . . Serve with Parmesan cheese. . . . Cut vegetables in julienne strips and cook in soup. . . . Add cooked peas or green beans just before serving. . . . Add thin slices of avocado just before serving. . . . Add thinly sliced raw mushrooms to soup just before serving. . . . Flavor consomme with a small amount of sherry. . . . Serve clear, well seasoned consomme with a poached egg in the soup dish.

WATERCRESS SOUP

2 bunches watercress, washed and cut up
4 potatoes, peeled and cut up
1 tablespoon salt
6 cups water
1 cup milk
1 tablespoon butter
6 slices French bread, dried in a slow oven

1. In a large saucepan combine watercress, potatoes, salt and water. Bring to a boil. Cover and simmer 30 minutes or until vegetables are well cooked.
2. Strain vegetables, reserving liquid. Put vegetables through a strainer. Return puree to saucepan. Add liquid and bring to a boil.
3. Add milk and bring to the boiling point but do not allow to boil.
4. Butter slices of bread and place it in bottom of soup bowls. Pour soup over bread and serve.
5. Makes 4 servings.

VICHYSSOISE

6 or 7 leeks
2 small onions
3 tablespoons sweet butter
7 medium potatoes
6 cups water or chicken broth
1½ tablespoons salt
3 cups milk
3 cups medium cream
1½ cups heavy cream
Chives

1. Wash leeks and remove roots. Thinly slice just the white part of the leeks. Discard green tops.
2. Slice onions.
3. Melt butter in a large kettle. Add leeks and onions and cook until limp, but not browned.
4. Peel and slice potatoes. Add to leeks with water and salt. Bring to a boil and cook gently 35 to 40 minutes, or until potatoes are tender.
5. Rub leek and potato mixture through a fine strainer or whirl in a blender.
6. Return to heat and add milk and the medium cream. Add additional seasoning if necessary. Bring mixture just to the boiling point, but do not boil.
7. Cool. Rub through a very fine strainer. When soup is cold, stir in the heavy cream.
8. Chill thoroughly, several hours if necessary, before serving. Serve topped with finely chopped chives.
9. Makes about 12 servings.

Note: This will keep nicely in the refrigerator for several days.

COUNTRY SOUP

3 tablespoons butter
2 medium carrots, cleaned and sliced
3 leeks, white part only, cleaned and cut into small pieces
2 cups chopped cabbage
2 stalks celery, cut into 1-inch pieces
1 teaspoon salt
½ teaspoon sugar
1 quart water
3 cups beef bouillon
1 cup cooked white beans
2 medium potatoes, cubed
6 slices French bread fried in butter
Grated Swiss cheese

1. Melt butter in a large, heavy saucepan. Add carrots, leeks, cabbage and celery. Simmer over low heat, stirring occasionally, about 20 minutes.
2. Add salt, sugar, water and bouillon. Bring to a boil. Add beans and potatoes. Cover and simmer 45 minutes or until vegetables are tender.
3. Strain vegetables. Reserve liquid. Put vegetables through a strainer to make a puree. Put the puree back in the saucepan and stir in liquid. Season to taste and heat.
4. Serve over slices of fried bread in large soup bowls. Sprinkle with grated cheese.
5. Makes 4 to 6 servings.

BEAN SOUP

2 cups dried beans
Water
1 teaspoon salt
1 tablespoon butter or margarine
1 carrot, diced
2 leeks, minced
1 onion, chopped
¼ pound salt pork or 1 ham bone
2 sprigs parsley
1 stalk celery
½ bay leaf
Pinch of thyme
Grind of fresh pepper

1. Wash and pick over beans, discarding hulls and imperfect beans. Cover with water and let soak over night.
2. Drain beans. Cover with fresh water, about 1½ quarts, add salt and bring to a boil. Skim top of soup as beans boil.
3. Melt butter in a saucepan. Add carrots, leeks and onion and cook until golden brown. Add to beans. Add salt pork, parsley, celery, bay leaf, thyme and pepper. Reduce heat and simmer, covered, 1 to 2 hours or until beans are tender.
4. Remove salt pork and reserve. Remove parsley, celery and bay leaf and discard. Drain beans in a sieve, reserving liquid. Rub the beans through the sieve to make a puree. Return puree to soup pot. Add enough of the cooking liquid to make the soup the desired thickness. Season to taste. If soup is too thick, thin with a little milk.
5. Cut salt pork into tiny cubes. Serve soup hot topped with cubes of salt pork.
6. Makes 6 servings.

OXTAIL SOUP

¼ cup butter or margarine
2 pounds oxtails, cut in pieces
2 large carrots, peeled and sliced
1 medium turnip, peeled and diced
1 large onion, diced
2 stalks celery, sliced
1 large leek, sliced
2 veal knuckles
3 quarts beef consommé
¼ cup catsup
¼ cup dry sherry
    Salt and pepper

1. Melt butter in a large soup kettle. Add oxtails and cook until lightly browned on all sides. Remove oxtails and reserve.
2. Add carrots, turnip, onion, celery and leeks to melted butter in soup kettle. Cook, stirring, until vegetables are golden brown.
3. Return oxtails to soup pot. Add veal knuckles and beef consommé. Bring mixture to a boil and skim off top foam. Lower heat, cover tightly, and simmer about 3 hours.
4. Remove veal knuckles. Stir in catsup and dry sherry. Season to taste with salt and pepper. Simmer about 15 minutes to blend flavors.
5. Makes 12 servings.

CLASSIC FRENCH PÂTÉ

½ pound lean veal cut into ¼-inch strips
1 can (⅞ ounces) diced truffles
3 tablespoons Cognac
    Pinch of salt
    Grind of fresh pepper
    Pinch ot thyme
    Pinch of allspice
1 tablespoon minced shallots or green onions
½ cup finely minced onion
2 tablespoons butter
½ cup Madeira or Cognac
¾ pound (1½ cups) finely ground lean pork
¾ pound (1½ cups) finely ground lean veal
½ pound finely ground pork fat
2 eggs
1½ teaspoons salt
⅛ teaspoon pepper
    Pinch allspice
½ teaspoon thyme
1 clove garlic, mashed
    Fresh pork fat or fat salt pork cut into very thin sheets
½ pound lean boiled ham cut into ¼-inch strips
1 bay leaf

1. Combine in a bowl the veal strips, truffles and their juice, cognac, pinch of salt, pepper, thyme and allspice, and minced shallots. Let stand while preparing the ground meat mixture.
2. Cook onions slowly in butter until they are tender but not browned. When onions are tender, scrape into a large mixing bowl. Add Madeira or cognac to skillet in which onions were cooked and boil it down until it is reduced by half. Scrape into bowl.
3. Add ground pork, veal, pork fat, eggs, 1½ teaspoons salt, ⅛ teaspoon pepper, pinch allspice, ½ teaspoon thyme and garlic. Beat vigorously with a wooden spoon until mixture is thoroughly blended. At this point take a small spoonful of the mixture and fry in a small skillet. Taste and add additional seasoning if desired.
4. Place sheets of fresh pork fat between sheets of waxed paper and pound until it is ⅛-inch thick. If you can't get fresh pork fat, slice salt pork in ⅛-inch thick slices. Place pork slices in a saucepan. Cover with cold water. Bring to a boil and simmer 10 minutes. Rinse well in cold water and dry with paper towels. Line the bottom and sides of an 8-cup terrine, baking dish, casserole or loaf pan with pork fat.
5. Heat oven to 350°F.
6. Drain veal strips and reserve marinade. Beat marinade into ground meat mixture.
7. Put ⅓ of the ground meat mixture in bottom of mold. Cover with half the strips of veal and half the strips of ham. Place diced truffles down center of strips. Cover strips with second third of the ground meat mixture and the remaining veal and ham strips. Top with remaining ground meat mixture. Place bay leaf on top of mixture. Cover top of meat with a layer of pork fat.
8. Cover top of mold tightly with aluminum foil. Set mold in pan of hot water. The water should come halfway up the mold.
9. Bake 1½ to 2 hours. The pâté is done when it has shrunk slightly from the sides of the mold or when the fat runs clear when it is pierced with a sharp knife.
10. Remove pate from water pan. Place a heavy weight on top of the pâté to press it down while it is cooling. (Place a couple of bricks on top of foil, or place a smaller loaf pan on top and weight down with canned goods or other heavy objects.)
11. Allow to cool thoroughly then chill in the refrigerator before serving.
12. Pâté may be served right from the mold or turned out onto a platter. Cut into slices.
13. Makes about 18 slices.

PÂTÉ DE PÂQUES

(shown opposite)

  2 packages pie crust mix
  1 cup grated Bonbel or Port Salut cheese
  5 eggs
  ¼ cup water
  2 tablespoons butter
  1 large onion, minced
  1 garlic clove, mashed
1½ pounds ground lean veal
1½ pounds ground lean pork
  1 pound bulk sausage meat
  1 tablespoon salt
  ½ teaspoon pepper
  ½ teaspoon marjoram
  6 hard cooked eggs, halved

1. Mix together pie crust mix with ½ cup of the grated cheese. Beat 2 eggs well with ¼ cup water. Stir into pie crust mix and stir until dough makes a ball in the middle of the bowl. Turn out on a lightly floured board and knead until smooth and elastic.
2. Line a greased 13- by 4- by 2½-inch loaf pan with heavy duty aluminum foil, allowing foil to extend over edges of pan.
3. Roll out ⅔ of the pastry on a lightly floured board to a 20- by 11- inch oblong. Use pastry to line the bottom and sides of the pan, allowing excess pastry to extend over the edges of the pan. Let chill in refrigerator with remaining pastry while making filling.
4. Heat oven to 350°F.
5. Melt butter in a small skillet. Add onions and garlic and cook until tender, but not browned. Scrape mixture into a large mixing bowl.
6. Add veal, pork, sausage meat, salt, pepper and marjoram.
7. Beat 3 eggs and set aside ¼ cup of the eggs to use later. Add eggs to meat mixture and mix until smooth and well blended.
8. Spoon half of the mixture into the pastry lined pan. Top mixture with halved eggs. Sprinkle with remaining ½ cup grated cheese. Spread evenly with remaining meat mixture.
9. Turn pastry extending over sides of pan over the meat. Brush pastry with beaten egg.
10. Roll out remaining pastry on a lightly floured board and cut into a 13- by 4-inch oblong to fit top of pan. Put pastry on top and seal edges firmly. Brush top with

beaten egg and decorate top with cutouts from scraps of pastry. Brush again with beaten egg.
11. Bake 2 hours or until pastry is richly browned.
12. Cool for 20 minutes. Remove from pan by pulling up foil overhang. Place on a serving platter and remove foil.
13. Serve hot, cut in slices, as a luncheon dish.
14. To serve cold, as a first course for dinner, leave pate in pan and chill for several hours. Remove from pan and cut in thin slices.
15. Makes 10 to 12 luncheon servings.

COUNTRY STYLE PÂTÉ

  1 pound ground lean pork
  1 pound ground veal
  ½ cup finely chopped onion
  ½ cup finely snipped parsley
1½ teaspoons salt
  ½ teaspoon ground black pepper
  1 tablespoon Worcestershire sauce
  1 teaspoon basil leaves
  2 tablespoons dry sherry
  4 eggs, lightly beaten
  Small sour pickles

1. Heat oven to 375°F.
2. Place all ingredients in a large mixing bowl. Blend thoroughly with hands or a large wooden spoon.
3. Turn mixture into an ungreased 9- by 5- by 3-inch loaf pan.
4. Bake about 1 hour or until loaf is set.
5. Cool meat in baking pan. Turn out of pan, wrap in aluminum foil and refrigerate.
6. Cut in thin slices and serve with small sour pickles as a first course.
7. Makes 12 to 16 slices.

QUICK PÂTÉ

2 envelopes unflavored gelatine
½ cup cold water
2 cans condensed bouillon
6 tablespoons brandy
4 cans (4¾ ounces each) liver pâté
Ripe olives

1. Sprinkle gelatine over cold water in a saucepan. Place over moderate heat and stir until gelatine dissolves. Add bouillon and brandy.

2. Chill mixture in refrigerator until it is the consistency of unbeaten egg white. Add liver pâté and beat with a rotary beater until mixture is well blended and smooth.

3. Turn mixture into a 5-cup mold or loaf pan.

4. Chill until firm.

5. Unmold and garnish with ripe olives cut in fancy shapes with canapé cutters.

6. Makes 24 servings when served as an appetizer.

Woman's World Library

PÂTÉ EN CROÛTE

4 cups unsifted flour
Salt
Butter or margarine
Water
4 eggs
1 pound lean veal, cut into ¼-inch strips
½ cup chopped shallots
⅔ cup brandy
1 pound ground lean veal
¼ pound pork fat, finely chopped
1 teaspoon thyme
1 can (⅞ ounces) truffles, chopped
1 pound ground pork
⅛ teaspoon allspice
⅛ teaspoon pepper
½ pound cooked ham, cut into ½-inch strips
3 bay leaves
1 egg yolk
1 envelope unflavored gelatine
2 cans (10½ ounces each) condensed beef consommé, undiluted

1. In a large bowl combine flour and 1 teaspoon salt. With a pastry blender or 2 knives cut in ⅔ cup butter, until mixture resembles coarse crumbs.

2. In a bowl combine ⅔ cup water and 2 eggs. Beat with a fork until well blended. Pour into flour mixture and stir with a fork until combined. When mixture gets stiff, knead with the hands until well blended. Shape into a ball and wrap in waxed paper. Chill in the refrigerator for several hours.

3. In a small bowl combine veal strips, 1 tablespoon shallots and 2 tablespoons brandy. Mix well. Cover and refrigerate.

4. Melt 2 tablespoons butter in a small skillet. Add remaining shallots and cook until tender, about 3 minutes. Add remaining brandy and simmer over medium heat until mixture is reduced to ½ cup.

5. In a bowl combine ground veal, pork fat, the shallot-brandy mixture, 1½ teaspoons salt, and thyme. Blend well. In a small bowl, blend truffles into 1 cup of this mixture. Set aside.

6. To veal mixture in large bowl add ground pork, 2 eggs, allspice and pepper. Blend well and set aside.

7. Line the sides and bottom of a 9- by 5- by 3-inch loaf pan with a double thickness of heavy-duty aluminum foil, allowing a 1-inch overhang.

8. Roll out two-thirds of the chilled pastry on a lightly floured board into a 12- by 15-inch rectangle. Fit pastry into foil-lined pan. Trim pastry, leaving a ½ inch overhang.

9. Remove 1 cup of the ground veal-pork mixture and set aside. Turn remaining mixture into pastry-lined pan. Pat down to make a 1 inch layer over bottom and up two sides of pan.

10. Line sides and bottom of mixture with almost all of the veal strips, then with almost all of the ham strips. Fill center with the reserved veal-truffle mixture. Top with remaining ham strips, then remaining veal strips. If there is any brandy left from veal strips, pour over the top.

11. Spread the reserved veal-pork mixture over top, patting it into an even layer. Arrange bay leaves on top.

12. Heat oven to 350°F.

13. Roll out remaining pastry into a 12- by 8-inch rectangle. Beat egg yolks with 1 teaspoon water. With a pastry brush, brush egg mixture around pastry overhang on pan. Place rectangle of pastry on top of pan. Pinch pastry together at edges to seal. Trim off excess pastry.

14. Roll out pastry trimmings and cut into desired shapes. Brush top crust with egg mixture then place cutouts on top. Brush decorations with egg mixture. Cut two holes, ½ inch in diameter, in top crust for steam vents. Insert a meat thermometer through one steam vent into center of meat.

15. Bake about 2½ hours or until meat thermometer registers 180°F. If fat begins to boil out of meat, place a piece of foil on rack below pâté. Remove pâté to wire rack.

16. Combine gelatine and 1 can consommé in a small saucepan. Stir. Place over low heat, stirring constantly, until gelatine is dissolved. Remove from heat and stir in remaining can of consommé.

17. With a funnel or bulb baster, add some consommé mixture to pâté through steam vents. Keep adding more every 10 or 15 minutes as pâté cools at room temperature. When pâté is cool, place in refrigerator. Add consommé at intervals until it is all used. Refrigerate pâté overnight before serving.

18. To serve, loosen pastry and foil around sides and ends. Carefully lift out pate and peel off foil. Place on a serving platter. Cut in thin slices for serving.

19. Makes 12 servings.

Egg Entrees

A typical American breakfast consists of fruit, bacon and eggs, toast and coffee, while in France breakfast is generally limited to rolls and coffee. Eggs are saved for lunch or dinner. Because they use eggs as the feature of main meals, the French have created numberless ways of serving them.

Every French housewife has a repertoire of her family's favorite omelets. Soft cooked and poached eggs are used in a variety of dishes, often served cold as well as hot. And the famous soufflés appear both as main courses and as desserts.

CHEESE SOUFFLÉ

(shown opposite)

2 tablespoons butter
2 tablespoons flour
¾ cup milk
½ teaspoon salt
¼ teaspoon freshly ground black pepper
  Pinch of nutmeg
1 cup grated Swiss cheese
4 egg yolks
5 egg whites

1. Heat oven to 375°F.
2. Butter a 1½-quart soufflé dish.
3. Melt butter in a heavy saucepan over low heat. Stir in flour and cook 1 minute. Remove from heat.
4. Slowly stir in milk and seasonings. Cook, stirring constantly, until mixture boils and is smooth and thickened. Add Swiss cheese and stir over very low heat until cheese is melted.
5. Remove from heat and stir slowly into beaten egg yolks, blending well.
6. Beat egg whites until mixture stands in stiff peaks and is glossy but not dry. Fold half of the egg white mixture into cheese mixture, folding in until it is thoroughly blended. Fold in second half until it is incorporated but still may be a little rough and lumpy.
7. Turn mixture into prepared soufflé dish. Run the back of a knife around top of soufflé, about 1 inch from the edge, to make a "top hat" when soufflé is baked.
8. Bake 25 to 30 minutes or until lightly browned and puffed.
9. Serve immediately.
10. Makes 4 servings.

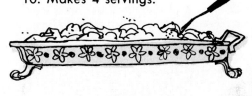

SOUFFLÉ PANCAKES

6 eggs, separated
⅓ cup buttermilk pancake mix
⅓ cup dairy sour cream
½ teaspoon salt

1. Beat egg yolks until thick and lemon colored. Fold in pancake mix, sour cream and salt.
2. Beat egg whites until stiff, but not dry. Carefully fold egg whites into yolk mixture.
3. Heat a griddle until hot. Grease the griddle well. Drop mixture by tablespoonfuls onto hot griddle. Bake until golden brown on both sides.
4. Serve piping hot with fresh fruit or honey.
5. Makes 6 servings.

Omelets

A good French omelet is a smooth, golden oval of perfectly cooked eggs. The omelet is cooked quickly so that the eggs are set on the outside and remain moist and creamy on the inside.

Every French household has a skillet used only for omelets. It is a heavy pan, from 7 to 8 inches across the bottom and with sloping sides. Because it is handled carefully and used only for omelets, it is never washed, merely wiped out after each use.

If you are buying an omelet pan, don't buy one larger than 7 or 8 inches as this is the perfect size for a 2 or 3 egg omelet. An aluminum or iron pan should be treated before using. Scrub the pan with steel wool and scouring powder. Rinse and dry. Heat for a minute or two until the bottom gets hot. Rub the bottom with cooking oil on a paper towel and let stand overnight. Before using it the first time, sprinkle the bottom with salt and rub vigorously; discard salt. After using, merely wipe out until the next use. Some of the new omelet pans are coated with Teflon and of course will present no problem of sticking.

For good omelets, the eggs should be out of the refrigerator for about 1 hour before cooking. The eggs should be beaten with a fork, only enough to blend the whites and yolks. Do not beat eggs with a whisk or beater. The pan should be preheated and is ready to use when the butter stops bubbling and is just beginning to turn slightly brown. Then the eggs are turned into the pan and very quickly made into an omelet. It takes practice and a little patience but it is well worth the effort.

OMELET

2 to 3 eggs
Pinch of salt
Small grind of pepper
1 tablespoon butter

1. Combine eggs, salt and pepper. Beat lightly with a fork, just until yolks and whites are combined.
2. Heat butter in omelet skillet over high heat just until it begins to turn brown.
3. Add eggs and immediately stir them briskly with a fork. When eggs have thickened, stop stirring. With left hand, shake the pan gently back and forth to loosen eggs and brown slightly.
4. Remove skillet from heat and tip it gently. With a fork, fold one third of omelet over center. Then fold other third over first. Slide omelet out of pan onto a heated serving dish.
5. Makes 1 to 2 servings.

Cheese Omelet: When eggs have just set, sprinkle 1 to 2 tablespoons grated Swiss cheese or Cheddar cheese over top and finish omelet as above.

Ham Omelet: Before cooking, fold 2 tablespoons minced cooked ham and a pinch of prepared mustard into beaten eggs.

Herb Omelet: Add ¼ teaspoon basil, thyme, oregano, or parsley flakes to egg before beating.

COUNTRY STYLE OMELET

2 tablespoons butter or margarine, divided
½ cup diced salt pork, bacon or ham
2 potatoes, partially cooked and finely diced
6 eggs
Chopped parsley
Chopped chives
Salt

1. Melt 1 tablespoon butter in omelet pan. Add salt pork and cook until salt pork is lightly browned. Remove salt pork.
2. Add potates to fat in pan and cook until potatoes are soft and lightly browned.
3. Beat eggs with a fork, just until yolks and whites are blended. Add a pinch of parsley, pinch of chives and a large pinch of salt.
4. Return salt pork to skillet with eggs. Stir quickly and thoroughly with a fork. When eggs start to set around edges, lift edges and put remaining butter around edges. Shake omelet pan gently to keep omelet from sticking. When lightly browned on the

bottom, flip over with a spatula, and brown second side lightly.
5. Serve piping hot.
6. Makes 3 to 4 servings.

OPEN FACED OMELET

6 slices bacon, cut into pieces
1 onion, thinly sliced
½ green pepper, thinly sliced
1 clove garlic, minced
1 teaspoon salt
Pinch of freshly ground black pepper
2 tomatoes, peeled and cut in pieces
10 eggs
2 tablespoons butter

1. Cook bacon in a large heavy skillet, until pieces are crispy and the fat has fried out. Remove bacon. Add onion, green pepper and garlic. Cook until tender but not browned.
2. Add salt, pepper and tomatoes. Simmer about 15 minutes or until tomatoes are tender.
3. Beat eggs with a fork, just until yolks and whites are mixed.
4. In a large skillet heat butter over high heat just until it begins to turn brown. Add eggs and stir briskly with a fork, just until eggs are set. When mixture is set and eggs are still moist let stand a few seconds to brown bottom Spread tomato mixture over surface. Sprinkle bacon over top.
5. Cut in pie-shaped wedges and serve immediately.
6. Makes 6 servings.

PUFFY CHEESE OMELET

6 eggs
½ teaspoon salt
Dash of pepper
½ cup grated Cheddar cheese, divided
1 tablespoon butter

1. Separate eggs into 2 large bowls.
2. Beat egg whites with a rotary beater until stiff but not dry.
3. Using same beater, without washing, beat egg yolks about 2 minutes. Fold in salt, pepper and ¼ cup cheese.
4. Pour yolk mixture over egg whites and fold into egg whites with a rubber scraper, until almost all the white is dispersed.
5. Heat butter in a large skillet over low heat.

6. Turn egg mixture into skillet and cook about 5 minutes. As eggs cook, lift outer edges up with a fork or spatula, so that the uncooked mixture can flow to bottom of pan. Cook until eggs are set and lightly browned on bottom and top has puffed a little, but is not dry. Top should still be moist.
7. Sprinkle remaining cheese over top. Place on broiler rack about 4 inches from source of heat and broil until top is puffy and lightly browned.
8. Cut into pie-shaped wedges for serving.
9. Makes 4 to 6 servings.

POACHED EGGS

1. Fill skillet about two-thirds full of water. Add 1 tablespoon salt and bring water to a boil. Reduce heat to simmering point.
2. Break each egg into a cup or saucer. Slip egg into water. Repeat, placing eggs side by side.
3. Cook 3 to 5 minutes or until whites are solid and yolks are done to desired degree of firmness.
4. Remove eggs with a slotted spoon or pancake turner.

EGGS BENEDICT

4 slices cooked ham, about ¼-inch thick, or Canadian bacon
2 English muffins
4 poached eggs
Quick Hollandaise Sauce

1. Brown ham slices or Canadian bacon in skillet over medium heat.
2. Split English muffins in half. Toast and butter lightly.
3. Poach eggs to desired degree of doneness.
4. Arrange ham on top of muffins. Top each with a poached egg. Cover with Hollandaise Sauce. Serve immediately.
5. Makes 2 dinner or luncheon servings.

Note: In France, Eggs Benedict are often served in flaky pastry shells rather than over muffins.

QUICK HOLLANDAISE SAUCE

½ cup butter or margarine
1 egg
2 tablespoons lemon juice
¼ teaspoon salt
Pinch of cayenne pepper

1. Melt butter in top of double boiler over hot, *not boiling*, water.
2. Add egg, lemon juice, salt and cayenne. Beat with a wire whisk until mixture is thick.
3. Remove at once from hot water. Serve over eggs.
4. Makes ¾ cup sauce.

EGGS BOURGUIGNONNE

2 cups dry light red wine
2 shallots, minced
1 bay leaf
Pinch of thyme
1 teaspoon salt
Pinch of pepper
1 sprig parsley
4 tablespoons butter, divided
Clove of garlic
8 slices French bread
8 eggs
1 tablespoon flour

1. Combine wine, shallots, bay leaf, thyme, salt, pepper and parsley in a skillet. Bring to a boil. Lower heat and simmer 15 minutes.
2. Melt 3 tablespoons butter in another large skillet. Rub cut piece of garlic over slices of French bread. Fry bread in butter until golden brown on both sides.
3. Break eggs, one by one, into a saucer and slide into wine sauce. Simmer to the desired degree of doneness, or until whites are firm and yolk is still soft. Spoon liquid over top of eggs as they poach.
4. Place fried bread on serving dishes. Place one poached egg on top of each slice of bread. Keep warm.
5. Bring wine mixture to a boil. Blend together remaining tablespoon of butter with flour. Mix to a paste. Stir into boiling wine. Cook and stir until slightly thickened. Taste for seasoning. When cooked down a little and slightly thickened, pour over eggs.
6. Makes 4 servings.

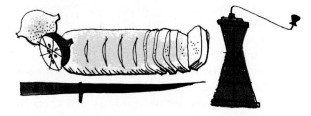

EGGS MORNAY

2 tablespoons butter or margarine
2 tablespoons flour
½ teaspoon salt
Grind of fresh pepper
½ teaspoon paprika
Dash of Tabasco
Dash of Worcestershire sauce
1½ teaspoons prepared mustard
2 cups milk
½ cup grated Swiss cheese
6 eggs

1. Heat oven to 400°F.
2. Melt butter in a small saucepan over medium heat. Stir in flour, salt, pepper, paprika, Tabasco and Worcestershire sauce. Cook 1 minute. Remove from heat and stir in mustard and milk. Return to heat and cook, stirring constantly, until sauce is smooth and thickened. Stir in cheese and mix until smooth.
3. Pour a thin layer of sauce into 3 well-greased individual baking dishes. Slip 2 eggs into each dish. Pour remaining sauce over tops of eggs, leaving yolks partially uncovered.
4. Bake 15 to 20 minutes or until eggs are of desired doneness.
5. Makes 3 servings.

EGGS COCOTTE

3 tablespoons butter
½ cup coarsely chopped mushrooms
Pinch of cayenne pepper
1 teaspoon flour
¼ cup chicken bouillon
½ teaspoon salt, divided
4 eggs

1. Heat oven to 400°F.
2. In a small skillet heat 1 tablespoon butter. Add mushrooms and cook over high heat, stirring constantly, for 2 minutes. Add cayenne and flour and cook until lightly browned. Stir in chicken bouillon and ¼ teaspoon salt. Lower heat and simmer 5 minutes.
3. Butter 4 small baking dishes or custard cups with remaining butter. Place 1 tablespoon of the mushroom mixture in bottom of each dish. Break 1 egg in each cup over mushrooms. Sprinkle with remaining salt.
4. Place cups in a pan of hot water. Bake about 10 minutes or until whites are well set. Serve immediately.
5. Makes 4 servings.

FLUFFY SHIRRED EGGS

4 eggs
¾ teaspoon salt
4 slices toast

1. Heat oven to 350°F.
2. Separate eggs, keeping each yolk separate in a custard cup.
3. Add salt to egg whites. Beat until stiff but not dry.
4. Trim crusts from toast slices and place on a baking sheet. Pile egg whites on top of toast slices. With a spoon make a well in center of whites. Slip an egg yolk into each well.
5. Bake 10 to 12 minutes or until yolks are baked to desired degree of consistency.
6. Makes 2 to 4 servings.

SHIRRED EGGS WITH BACON

4 slices Canadian bacon
2 thin slices Swiss cheese, cut into 2 pieces
4 eggs
½ teaspoon salt
¼ teaspoon white pepper
¼ cup dairy sour cream

1. Heat oven to 400°F.
2. Place bacon in bottom of an 8-inch pie plate. Place slices of cheese over bacon. Break eggs on top of cheese.
3. Combine salt, pepper and sour cream. Spoon over tops of eggs.
4. Bake 15 to 20 minutes or until whites of eggs are set. Serve from dish.
5. Makes 4 servings.

SCRAMBLED EGGS

8 eggs
¾ teaspoon salt
⅛ teaspoon pepper
½ cup milk or light cream
2 tablespoons butter or margarine

1. Combine eggs, salt, pepper and milk in a mixing bowl. Beat with a fork, just until yolks and whites are blended.
2. Melt butter in a large skillet, tilting skillet so that bottom and sides are covered.
3. Pour in eggs and reduce heat to moderately low. Cook slowly, stirring gently with a wooden spoon. Cook just until eggs are set and still moist.
4. Serve immediately on heated plates.
5. Makes 4 servings.

EGGS BEURRE NOIR

2 tablespoons butter
4 eggs
1 teaspoon wine vinegar

1. Heat butter in a medium skillet. Let butter brown without burning.
2. When it is dark in color, break eggs into the pan and fry until whites are thoroughly cooked.
3. Remove the eggs to a heated platter. Add vinegar to heated butter in pan, stir 1 minute and then pour over eggs.
4. Makes 2 servings.

EGGS COOKED IN THE SHELL

1. Have unshelled eggs at room temperature. Place in a saucepan and add enough cold water to cover eggs by at least 1 inch.
2. Cover saucepan and bring to a rapid boil.
3. Remove from heat; if cooking more than 4 eggs, let stand over very low heat. Let stand covered:
   Very soft cooked eggs, 2 minutes
   Medium soft cooked eggs, 3½ minutes
   Firm soft cooked eggs, about 4 minutes
   Hard cooked eggs, 15 minutes.
4. Run cold water over eggs as soon as cooking time is up to stop further cooking and make them easier to handle.

EGGS EN GELÉE

6 eggs
Boiling water
2 envelopes unflavored gelatine
2 cans (12½ ounces each) chicken consommé
½ cup dry white wine
1 tablespoon tarragon vinegar
¾ teaspoon salt
12 fresh tarragon leaves
4 tablespoons liver pâté
1 teaspoon heavy cream

1. Gently lower eggs into boiling water in a medium saucepan. Remove from heat. Cover and let stand 5 minutes. Cool eggs immediately in cold water to prevent further cooking.
2. Soften gelatine in 1 can of the consommé in a small sauce pan. Stir over low heat until gelatine is dissolved. Add remaining consommé, wine, vinegar and salt. Set aside.
3. Pour boiling water over tarragon leaves. Drain leaves and plunge in ice water.
4. Beat pâté with heavy cream until smooth.

Put mixture in a pastry bag fitted with small star tip.
5. Spoon 1 tablespoon gelatine mixture into 6 oval molds or custard cups. Refrigerate 5 minutes or until gelatine is just set, not firm. Arrange 2 tarragon leaves on gelatine in each mold. Pipe liver pâté in a design around tarragon leaves. Carefully cover with a thin layer of gelatine. Chill until gelatine is set.
6. Peel eggs. Place 1 egg in the center of each mold or custard cup on top of gelatine. Pour remaining gelatine mixture around the eggs to cover them.
7. Refrigerate molds. If there is any gelatine left, pour into a shallow pan and refrigerate with eggs.
8. Unmold eggs onto individual serving dishes. Chop any remaining gelatine and place around eggs. Garnish with parsley.
9. Makes 6 servings.

GARLIC EGGS

2 cloves garlic
12 filets of anchovy
6 capers
3 tablespoons olive oil
1 teaspoon wine vinegar
½ teaspoon salt
⅛ teaspoon freshly ground black pepper
6 hard cooked eggs

1. Crush garlic cloves. Add anchovies and capers and mash together to make a paste. Stir in oil, vinegar, salt and pepper.
2. Peel eggs and cut in quarters. Cover eggs with sauce.
3. Makes 4 to 6 servings.

STUFFED EGGS

4 hard cooked eggs
2 tablespoons crumbled Roquefort cheese
1 teaspoon prepared mustard
1 teaspoon snipped chives
½ teaspoon rosemary
2 tablespoons mayonnaise
Salt and pepper
Paprika

1. Peel eggs. Split lengthwise and remove yolks.
2. Combine yolks with cheese, mustard, chives, rosemary and mayonnaise. Blend well. Season to taste with salt and pepper.
3. Use mixture to fill egg whites. Sprinkle a bit of paprika on top of each egg.
4. Makes 8 filled egg halves.

Fish and Shellfish

France is a country lapped by oceans on three sides and crossed by a multitude of rivers, both big and small. This means there is a plentiful supply of fish and shellfish, enough to please everyone's taste. They are the proud possessors of several varieties of oysters, which come from the ocean so delightfully seasoned that they need only a squirt of lemon to please the most jaded palate. Here in America the mussel is all but ignored but in France it becomes a gourmet's delight.

Because fish is so abundant and varied, the French have evolved many ways of cooking it. A simple piece of freshly caught, fried or broiled fish is delicious, cooked to perfection, but they have gone a step farther to concoct fish dishes poached or baked in wine sauces. Simple filets are topped with delightful cream and mushroom sauces. Cold poached fish, topped with mayonnaise, is a summer's delight. And best of all, the great fish dish that everyone raves about, the combination of many fishes, called bouillabaisse.

VERMOUTH-POACHED FISH FILETS
(shown opposite)

> 1 bunch scallions
> 1½ pounds fish filets, flounder, sole or perch
> 1 teaspoon salt
> Grind of fresh pepper
> 1 teaspoon dried dill weed or tarragon
> Dry vermouth
> ¼ cup toasted slivered almonds

1. Heat oven to 350°F.
2. Trim scallions. Slice white bulbs and 3 inches of green stalks. Spread scallions in a shallow, buttered baking dish. Arrange fish filets in a single layer over scallions. Sprinkle with salt, pepper and dill or tarragon. Pour enough vermouth into baking dish to just cover filets.
3. Cover with a lid or a piece of aluminum foil. Bake 15 minutes. Remove lid and bake 5 minutes longer or until fish flakes easily when tested with a fork.
4. Scatter almonds over surface just before serving.
5. Makes 4 servings.

FISH FILETS

> 2 tablespoons finely chopped onion
> 1 medium carrot, cleaned and chopped
> 1 lemon, sliced
> Pinch of thyme
> 1 small bay leaf
> 1 teaspoon salt
> ¼ teaspoon pepper
> 1 to 1½ pounds fish filets
> 1 cup dry white wine
> 2 tablespoons vermouth
> 1 tablespoon chopped parsley

1. Heat oven to 400°F.
2. Place onion, carrot, lemon, thyme, bay leaf, salt and pepper in a greased shallow baking dish. Place filets on top of vegetables. Combine wine and vermouth and pour over fish.

3. Bake 20 minutes or until fish flakes easily when tested with a fork.
4. Sprinkle with parsley and serve with juices in baking dish.
5. Makes 4 to 6 servings.

ALMOND FISH FILETS

> 1 medium onion, sliced
> 1 bay leaf
> 4 fish filets
> ¼ teaspoon salt
> Grind of fresh pepper
> Pinch of thyme
> ¼ cup blanched slivered almonds
> 1 tablespoon salad oil
> 1 small onion, grated
> 1 teaspoon grated lemon peel
> 1 tablespoon snipped parsley
> 1 tablespoon white wine
> 1 chicken bouillon cube
> ¼ cup boiling water

1. Heat oven to 350°F.
2. Place onion slices and bay leaf in a shallow baking dish. Season fish filets with salt, pepper and thyme. Place on top of onion slices.
3. In a small skillet, brown almonds lightly in hot oil. Add onion and cook about 1 minute. Stir in lemon rind, parsley and wine. Dissolve bouillon cube in boiling water and add to sauce. Blend thoroughly and pour over fish.
4. Bake 15 to 20 minutes or until fish flakes easily when tested with a fork.
5. Makes 4 servings.

FISH DUGLÈRE

4 fish filets
1 teaspoon salt
Grind of fresh pepper
5 tablespoons butter or margarine, divided
1 medium onion, chopped
1 clove garlic
4 ripe tomatoes, peeled and chopped
1 tablespoon snipped parsley
¼ cup dry white wine
½ cup water
1 tablespoon flour

1. Season filets with salt and pepper. Melt 3 tablespoons of butter in a large skillet. Add onions and garlic and cook gently until onions are soft.
2. Place filets in pan. Arrange tomatoes and parsley over fish. Add wine and water. Cover with a circle of waxed paper, cut to fit within pan, with a hole in the center. Cover tightly and simmer over medium low heat about 8 minutes or until fish flakes easily when tested with a fork.
3. Remove fish to a hot platter. Boil liquid until it is reduced to ⅓ its original quantity. Remove garlic.
4. Cream together flour and remaining 2 tablespoons butter. Stir into mixture in skillet and cook, stirring, until mixture comes to a boil and is thickened. Pour sauce over fish.
5. Makes 4 servings.

SOLE BELLE AURORE

6 filets of sole or flounder
3 tablespoons butter
1 tablespoon minced onion
½ cup clam juice
Pinch of salt
Grind of fresh pepper
½ cup non-dairy powdered cream
3 tablespoons flour
1 cup boiling water
¼ cup minced parsley

1. Halve the filets lengthwise; roll and tie with thread or secure with toothpicks.
2. Melt butter in a skillet over medium heat. Add onion and cook just until very lightly browned. Add filets and cook until lightly browned.
3. Add clam juice, salt and pepper. Bring just to the boil. Lower heat and simmer 10 minutes or until filets flake easily when tested with a fork.
4. Remove fish to a shallow casserole. Combine powdered cream and flour. Blend into

hot liquid in skillet. Blend in boiling water. Cook over medium heat, stirring constantly, until mixture thickens. Stir in parsley and pour sauce over fish in casserole.
5. Preheat broiler. Place casserole under broiler and brown lightly.
6. Makes 6 servings.

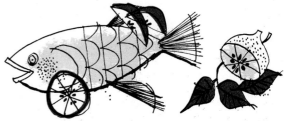

FILETS DE SOLE VÉRONIQUE

6 filets of sole, about ¼-pound each
2 tablespoons butter
2 tablespoons chopped onion
1 teaspoon salt
⅛ teaspoon pepper
¾ cup dry white wine, divided
1 tablespoon softened butter
4 teaspoons flour
⅓ cup instant non-fat dry milk
1 cup seedless green grapes

1. Heat oven to 350°F.
2. Pat sole dry with paper toweling. Spread bottom of a shallow casserole with butter. Sprinkle onion in bottom of dish. Season sole with salt and pepper. Roll each filet and skewer with toothpicks. Place in casserole on top of onion. Pour ½ cup wine over fish.
3. Cover the casserole with a piece of waxed paper, cut to fit down over the top of the fish. Bake 20 minutes or until fish flakes easily when tested with a fork.
4. Remove filets and place on a heat-proof platter and keep warm. Remove toothpicks.
5. Drain liquid from fish into a small saucepan. Work together the softened butter and flour into a paste. Stir into the fish stock and cook over medium heat, stirring, until mixture is smooth. Stir in dry milk and remaining ¼ cup wine. Cook, stirring constantly, until thickened.
6. Pour sauce over filets on the heat-proof platter. Arrange grapes around fish filets. Place under preheated broiler and broil about 1 minute or until the sauce bubbles.
7. Makes 6 servings.

Filet of Sole Véronique is a dish any cook would be proud to serve. Sole, poached in white wine and garnished with grapes, makes a company dinner.

American Dairy Association

FILET OF SOLE IN WHITE WINE

        1 bottle (7½ ounces) clam juice
        ½ cup dry white wine
        ½ bay leaf
        6 whole peppercorns
        ½ teaspoon salt
          Sprig of parsley
        1 clove garlic, split
          Water
        2 pounds filet of sole
          Lemon juice
        2 tablespoons butter
        2 tablespoons flour

1. Combine clam juice, wine, bay leaf, peppercorns, salt, parsley, garlic and ½ cup water in a saucepan. Bring to a boil. Reduce heat and simmer, uncovered, 15 minutes.
2. Heat oven to 350°F.
3. Sprinkle filets with lemon juice. Fold each filet into thirds. Arrange in a single layer in a shallow baking dish.
4. Strain clam mixture over filets. Cover dish tightly with aluminum foil.
5. Bake 15 minutes or until fish flakes easily when tested with a fork.
6. Carefully remove filets to a warm serving platter. Keep warm. Reserve 1 cup of the liquid from the baking dish.
7. Melt butter in a saucepan. Stir in flour. Remove from heat and stir in fish liquid. Return to heat and cook over medium heat, stirring constantly, until smooth and thickened. Taste for seasoning. Add a little lemon juice if needed.
8. Serve with poached fish.
9. Makes 6 servings.

BAKED SOLE MOUSSE

        3 cups cooked flaked sole or flounder
          (about 1½ pounds)
        3 egg whites, slightly beaten
        1 teaspoon salt
        ½ teaspoon paprika
          Grind of fresh pepper
          Non-dairy powdered cream
        1½ cups boiling water
        2 cans (4 ounces each) sliced mushrooms,
          drained
        3 tablespoons butter or margarine
        2 tablespoons water

1. Heat oven to 350°F.
2. Combine cooked flaked fish, beaten egg whites, salt, paprika, pepper, 1½ cups non-dairy powdered cream and boiling wa-

ter. Mix well. Pour mixture into a lightly buttered 1½ -quart fish mold or casserole. Place mold in a pan of hot water. Bake 45 to 50 minutes or until mixture is set.
3. Sauté well drained mushrooms in butter in a small skillet. Combine 2 tablespoons non-dairy powdered cream with 2 tablespoons water. Stir into mushrooms and bring just to the boil.
4. Unmold mousse on a hot serving platter. Serve with mushroom sauce.
5. Makes 6 to 8 servings.

SOLE IN MOUSSELINE SAUCE

        6 filets of sole
          Salt
          Pepper
        ½ cup dry white wine
        3 egg yolks
          Dash cayenne pepper
        ½ cup butter
        ¼ cup heavy cream

1. Heat oven to 400°F.
2. Wipe filets with paper toweling. Sprinkle with salt and pepper and roll up each filet. Secure with toothpicks.
3. Heat wine in a skillet with a dash of salt. Add sole, cover and simmer slowly for about 5 minutes, or until fish is opaque. Remove sole to a baking dish.
4. Boil down wine to 2 tablespoonsful; strain into blender container. Add egg yolks, a pinch of salt and cayenne pepper. Turn blender on for a few seconds. Heat butter until it is foaming hot. Turn on blender, remove cover and slowly pour in butter. Turn sauce out of blender and cool slightly. Whip cream until stiff and fold into cooled sauce. Spoon over poached filets.
5. Bake 10 minutes or until thoroughly heated.
6. Makes 6 servings.

Note: To prepare sauce without a blender, combine egg yolks, reduced wine, salt and cayenne pepper in a small saucepan. Cook over hot, *not boiling,* water, stirring constantly until slightly thickened. Melt butter and beat in a little at a time, beating constantly with a wire whisk. Then cool and fold in whipped cream.

SALMON SAINT-JACQUES

1 can (1 pound) salmon
1 cup light cream
2 tablespoons dry white wine
3 tablespoons butter or margarine
2 tablespoons minced onion
3 tablespoons flour
½ teaspoon salt
⅛ teaspoon pepper
1 teaspoon Ac'cent
1 egg yolk, beaten
1 teaspoon snipped parsley
¾ cup fine bread crumbs
2 tablespoons melted butter or margarine
2 tablespoons grated Parmesan cheese

1. Heat oven to 425°F.
2. Drain salmon. Combine salmon liquid, cream and wine. Set aside.
3. Melt butter in a saucepan; add onion and cook until transparent. Stir in flour, salt, pepper and Ac'cent. Gradually stir in reserved salmon liquid mixture. Cook, stirring constantly, until mixture thickens and comes to a boil.
4. Stir a small amount of hot mixture into beaten egg yolk. Return to mixture in saucepan. Cook over low heat, stirring constantly, for 1 minute. Remove from heat.
5. Fold in salmon and parsley. Spoon mixture into 4 individual baking dishes. Combine bread crumbs, butter and Parmesan cheese. Sprinkle over top of salmon.
6. Bake 5 minutes or until crumbs are lightly browned.
7. Makes 4 servings.

FISH STEAKS IN WHITE WINE

6 tablespoons butter, divided
4 salmon or swordfish steaks
1 cup dry white wine or sherry
Salt and pepper
2 teaspoons chopped parsley
1 teaspoon lemon juice

1. Melt 4 tablespoons butter in a skillet over medium heat. When foam subsides, add salmon steaks and brown lightly on both sides.
2. Add wine and season with salt and pepper. Cook quickly until about three-fourths of the liquid is absorbed. When fish flakes easily with a fork, it is done.
3. Remove to a hot serving platter. Blend together 2 tablespoons butter, parsley and lemon juice. Spread over fish and serve immediately.
4. Makes 4 servings.

SUMMER FISH STEAKS

1 tablespoon olive oil
1 to 1½ pounds sword fish or salmon steaks, cut in 4 to 6 pieces.
4 tomatoes, peeled and chopped
Pinch of fennel
Pinch of thyme
1 small bay leaf
1 clove garlic, crushed
4 peppercorns
½ teaspoon salt
¼ teaspoon saffron
1 cup dry white wine
1 lemon, cut in thin slices

1. Heat oil in a large skillet. Tip skillet so oil covers bottom of pan.
2. Place fish steaks in skillet. Add tomatoes, fennel, thyme, bay leaf, garlic, peppercorns, salt and saffron. Pour wine over the top.
3. Bring mixture to a boil. Cover and simmer over low heat 10 minutes or until fish flakes easily when tested with a fork. *Do not overcook.*
4. Cool fish in cooking liquid. Chill until cold.
5. Serve fish cold with 4 to 6 tablespoons of cooking liquid. Garnish with thin slices of lemon.
6. Makes 4 to 6 servings.

SEAFOOD MÉDITERANNÉE

½ cup olive oil
3 cloves garlic, minced
6 small rock lobster tails, cut in thirds
1 teaspoon oregano
1½ teaspoons salt
½ teaspoon pepper
1 can (1 pound) Italian plum tomatoes
1 cup dry white wine
2 bay leaves
1½ dozen cherrystone clams, scrubbed
1 pound shrimp, cleaned and deveined
1 cup snipped parsley

1. Heat olive oil in a Dutch oven. Add garlic and cook, stirring, for 1 minute. Add lobster pieces and cook, stirring, for 3 minutes.
2. Add oregano, salt, pepper, tomatoes, wine and bay leaves. Blend thoroughly and bring to a boil. Cover and simmer 5 minutes.
3. Add clams, shrimp, and parsley. Bring mixture to a boil. Reduce heat, cover, and cook 5 minutes or until shrimp are cooked and the clams are open.
4. Serve in soup bowls with French bread.
5. Makes 4 to 6 servings.

BOUILLABAISSE MARSEILLAISE

1 pound cleaned red snapper
1 pound perch, cleaned
1 pound cod
1 pound eel
1½ pounds striped bass
2½ pounds mackerel
2 medium sized lobsters or 4 lobster tails
3 large leeks, cleaned and cut in chunks
2 medium onions, chopped
1 carrot, peeled and chopped
1 pound fresh tomatoes, peeled and chopped
2 cloves garlic, crushed
2 tablespoons snipped parsley
1 teaspoon saffron
1 bay leaf
Pinch thyme
Pinch chopped fresh fennel
Grated rind of ½ orange
1 teaspoon salt
Dash of pepper
Water
½ cup olive oil

1. Cut snapper, perch, cod, eel, bass and mackerel into 1-inch slices. Cut lobsters in half, remove vein. Cut tail section into chunks, including shell. Crack lobster claws and break into sections.
2. In a large kettle combine leeks, onions, carrot, tomatoes, garlic, parsley, saffron, bay leaf, thyme, fennel, orange rind, salt and pepper. Cover mixture with water. Bring to a boil and simmer 5 minutes. Add fish, except perch and cod. Pour olive oil over top and add more water, if needed, to cover. Bring to a boil and boil rapidly for 8 minutes.
3. Add perch and cod. Boil rapidly 8 more minutes.
4. You may serve the soup and fish separately. Or serve both together in large soup bowls, with lots of French bread.
5. Makes 10 to 12 servings.

CHAFING DISH CRAB MEAT

3 tablespoons butter
4 large mushrooms, sliced
2 teaspoons finely chopped shallots
2 tablespoons tomato paste
1¼ cups heavy cream, divided
1 pound fresh, canned or frozen lump crab meat, picked over but not broken up
Salt and pepper
2 egg yolks
1 teaspoon snipped parsley
1 teaspoon snipped chives
Pinch of tarragon
¼ cup cognac
Hot cooked rice

1. Have ingredients all measured out and ready on a tray if preparing this in a chafing dish at the table.
2. Melt butter in chafing dish or electric skillet. Add mushrooms and cook about 5 minutes, stirring.
3. Add shallots and cook until liquid from mushrooms has disappeared. Stir in tomato paste and cook a few minutes.
4. Stir in 1 cup cream and cook, stirring constantly, until mixture begins to simmer and is well blended.
5. Add crab meat. Season to taste with salt and pepper. Stir gently and heat well.
6. Beat together the egg yolks and ¼ cup cream. Stir this mixture slowly into crab meat mixture. Add parsley, chives and tarragon. Heat, stirring constantly, until mixture is hot. *Do not boil.*
7. Stir in cognac. Serve immediately over hot cooked rice or keep warm over hot water if serving for a buffet.
8. Makes 6 servings.

CRAB MEAT EN RAMEKIN

2 tablespoons butter or margarine
2 tablespoons flour
1 tablespoon prepared mustard
½ teaspoon Worcestershire sauce
Few drops Tabasco
¼ teaspoon nutmeg
½ cup milk
½ cup heavy cream
2 egg yolks, slightly beaten
¼ cup dry white wine
3 cups picked over crab meat
Buttered bread crumbs

1. Heat oven to 400°F.
2. Melt butter in a heavy saucepan. Stir in flour and cook 1 minute, stirring constantly. Remove from heat.
3. Stir in mustard, Worcestershire sauce, Tabasco and nutmeg. Stir in milk and

cream. Cook over low heat, stirring constantly, until mixture is smooth and thickened.

4. Stir a little of the hot sauce into beaten egg yolks. Return egg mixture to remaining sauce and cook over very low heat 1 minute.
5. Fold in wine and crab meat. Fill 4 to 6 ramekins with crab meat mixture. Top with buttered bread crumbs.
6. Bake 10 minutes or until heated through and lightly browned on top.
7. Makes 4 to 6 servings.

SHRIMP AU GRATIN

   2 pounds shrimp, shelled and cleaned
   2 cups dry white wine
  ½ cup butter, divided
   1 pound fresh mushrooms, chopped
  ¼ cup chopped onion
  ¼ cup flour
  ¼ cup heavy cream
   1 teaspoon salt
  ¼ teaspoon pepper
   1 cup crushed saltines

1. Combine shrimp and wine in a saucepan and simmer gently about 5 minutes, or until shrimp are no longer translucent. Drain shrimp, reserving hot wine.
2. Melt ¼ cup butter in a saucepan. Cook mushrooms and onion in hot butter until lightly browned. Blend in flour. Remove from heat and slowly add 2 cups of the hot wine in which shrimp were cooked. Cook over low heat, stirring constantly, until smooth and thick. Stir in cream. Season with salt and pepper.
3. Add shrimp to hot sauce. Divide mixture into 8 individual ramekins. Sprinkle crushed saltines over the top. Use remaining butter to dot top of each ramekin.
4. Preheat broiler. Place ramekins about 4 inches from source of heat and cook until lightly browned on top.
5. Makes 8 servings.

QUENELLES WITH SEAFOOD SAUCE

   6 frozen pastry shells or toast shells
   1 can (14½ ounces) lobster bisque
  ½ can water
   1 can (4 ounces) shrimp, drained
  ½ teaspoon salt
    Grind of fresh black pepper
   1 can (10¾ ounces) Quenelles de Brochet (Pike Dumplings)
   1 teaspoon lemon juice

1. Bake patty shells according to directions on package.
2. If you prefer toast shells, trim crust from slices of bread. Fit slices of bread into cupcake pans. Brush surface with melted butter. Toast in a moderately hot oven (375° F.) 10 to 15 minutes or until lightly browned. Cool in pan and remove carefully.
3. Combine lobster bisque and water. Beat with a rotary beater until smooth. Heat to the boiling point. Add shrimp, salt and pepper. Cut quenelles in halves and add to sauce. Heat thoroughly, but do not boil. Stir very carefully so that quenelles will hold their shape. Fold in lemon juice.
4. Serve piping hot in pastry shells or toast shells.
5. Makes 4 servings.

MUSSELS IN WINE

   3 dozen mussels
   1 cup dry white wine
   1 cup heavy cream
   1 medium onion, finely chopped
  ¼ cup snipped parsley
   2 tablespoons butter
  ½ teaspoon salt
  ¼ teaspoon cayenne pepper

1. Check mussels, discarding any that are not tightly closed. Scrub well under cold running water to remove sand, seaweed and barnacles. A stiff brush or steel wool works very nicely. With a sharp knife, trim off beard around the edges. Place mussels in a large bowl and cover with cold water. Let stand 1 to 2 hours.
2. Drain mussels. Put in a large kettle with the wine, cream, onion, parsley, butter, salt and cayenne pepper.
3. Cover tightly and bring to a boil. Continue cooking for 3 minutes or until flesh of mussels turn white.
4. Serve mussels covered with juice in large flat soup bowls. Serve with French bread to mop up the juice.
5. Makes 4 servings.

ROCK LOBSTER À LA BORDELAISE

¼ cup butter or margarine, divided
2 medium carrots, peeled and diced
1 small onion, chopped
4 rock lobster tails (4 to 6 ounces each)
1 tablespoon olive oil
½ teaspoon salt
   Pinch of cayenne pepper
½ cup dry white wine
3 tablespoons tomato paste
2 tablespoons bottled clam juice
1 bouillon cube

1. Melt 2 tablespoons butter in a small saucepan. Add carrots and onions and simmer over low flame about 20 minutes, stirring
2. Cut lobster tails in 2-inch pieces.
3. Heat olive oil and 1 tablespoon butter in a heavy skillet. Add lobster pieces and cook over high heat, stirring, until lobster shells turn red. Add onion mixture, salt, cayenne pepper, wine, tomato paste, clam juice and bouillon cube. Bring to a boil. Cover and cook over medium heat 10 minutes.
4. Remove lobster from skillet to a heated serving dish and keep warm.
5. Simmer sauce left in skillet until it is reduced to about half its original volume. Remove skillet from heat. Add remaining tablespoon of butter in small bits, stirring until butter is melted and sauce is well blended. Pour sauce over lobster.
6. Makes 4 servings.

SOUTH AFRICAN ROCK LOBSTER THERMIDOR (shown opposite)

2 packages (9 ounces each) rock lobster tails
   Boiling water
1 tablespoon whole pickling spice
¼ cup butter or margarine
⅓ cup flour
1 can (10½ ounces) condensed chicken broth
¾ cup heavy cream
2 tablespoons sherry
1 tablespoon brandy
2 cans (4 ounces each) button mushrooms, drained
   Salt and pepper
¼ cup grated Parmesan cheese

1. Drop rock lobster tails into a large pot of boiling water to which pickling spice has been added. When water comes back to a boil, remove lobster and drench in cold water.
2. When lobster tails are cool, cut away un-

derside membrane of each tail and remove meat. Reserve shells. Dice lobster meat.
3. Melt butter in a saucepan over medium heat. Stir in flour and cook 1 minute. Remove from heat.
4. Gradually stir in chicken broth and cream. Add sherry and brandy. Cook over low heat, stirring constantly, until sauce comes to a boil and thickens.
5. Remove from heat and fold in mushrooms and diced lobster meat. Season to taste with salt and pepper.
6. Reheat thoroughly. Spoon mixture into reserved lobster shells. Sprinkle with Parmesan cheese.
7. Preheat broiling compartment. Broil lobster tails, about 4 inches from source of heat, until golden brown.
8. Makes 8 servings.

ROCK LOBSTER IN WHITE WINE SAUCE

8 rock lobster tails (4 ounces each)
   Boiling water
   Salt
4 tablespoons butter
4 tablespoons flour
2 cups milk
½ cup heavy cream
2 packages (3 ounces each) cream cheese
1 jar (3 ounces) pimiento, chopped
2 tablespoons snipped parsley
2 tablespoons scraped onion
½ teaspoon salt
1 teaspoon paprika
2 egg yolks, slightly beaten
¼ cup dry white wine
   Hot cooked spaghetti

1. Drop frozen rock lobster tails into boiling salted water. When water comes back to a boil, cook for 2 minutes. Drain immediately and drench with cold water. Remove meat from shells and cut in small pieces.
2. Melt butter in a saucepan over low heat. Stir in flour and cook 1 minute. Remove from heat and slowly stir in milk and cream. Cook, stirring constantly, until sauce comes to a boil and thickens.
3. Mash cream cheese with a fork. Stir into hot sauce. Add pimiento, parsley, onion, salt and paprika.
4. Stir a little of the hot sauce into beaten egg yolks. Return mixture to sauce in saucepan. Cook over low heat, stirring constantly, for 1 minute.
5. Stir in wine and lobster. Heat thoroughly before serving over spaghetti.
6. Makes 6 servings.

SEAFOOD CRÊPES

1 cup plus 2 tablespoons sifted flour
Pinch of salt
3 eggs, beaten
1½ cups milk
1 tablespoon melted butter or margarine
1½ tablespoons cognac
Butter
Crab or Tuna Filling

1. Combine flour and salt in a bowl. Beat eggs and milk together. Stir into flour mixture and beat until smooth. This can be done on low speed of a mixer or with a wire whisk. Stir in melted butter and cognac. Let mixture stand for 2 hours before cooking.
2. Heat a small frying pan, about 5¼ inches in diameter across the bottom, over medium high heat.
3. When skillet is hot, add ½ teaspoon butter and swirl around pan to cover sides and bottom. Pour in 1 full tablespoon batter. Rotate and tilt pan quickly to spread batter over bottom of skillet. This must be done quickly before batter has a chance to set.
4. Cook crêpe about 1 minute or until it is set and brown on one side. Loosen sides with spatula and flip crêpe over quickly with the fingers. Lightly brown second side. The second side will not brown as nicely as the first side, so it is usually turned inside when it is rolled around a filling.
5. Make crêpes and stack in a pile as they are baked. They may be used immediately, or made early in the day and filled just before serving. They may also be frozen, with a piece of waxed paper between each crêpe.
6. Fill with desired filling and procede as in given recipe.
7. Makes 20 to 24 5½-inch crêpes, or less if crêpes are larger.

CRAB FILLING

¼ cup butter or margarine
¼ cup flour
1½ cups milk
¼ cup dry sherry
½ cup chicken broth or bouillon
Salt
Pepper
1 egg yolk, beaten
½ cup heavy cream, divided
2 cups king crab meat, canned or frozen
1 can (3 ounces) chopped mushrooms, drained

1. Melt butter in a saucepan over medium heat. Blend in flour. Remove from heat and stir in milk, sherry and chicken broth. Cook over medium heat, stirring constantly, until smooth and thickened. Season to taste with salt and pepper.
2. Pour a little of cooked mixture over beaten egg. Return egg mixture to remaining sauce. Stir in ¼ cup cream. Cook over low heat 1 minute.
3. Reserve ½ cup of this sauce. Add crab meat and mushrooms to remaining sauce. Fill crêpes with crab mixture and roll up. Place fold side down in a heat-proof shallow baking dish.
4. Whip remaining ¼ cup cream. Fold into ½ cup of the reserved sauce. Spread mixture over crêpes.
5. Heat broiler. Run mixture under heat just long enough to brown lightly and glaze top of crêpes.
6. Makes 6 servings.

TUNA FILLING

½ cup butter or margarine, softened
3 egg yolks
⅓ cup boiling water
2 tablespoons lemon juice
Dash cayenne pepper
2 cans (6½ to 7 ounces each) chunk style tuna, drained
1 tablespoon minced parsley
½ cup grated Swiss cheese.

1. Soften the butter in top of a double boiler. Gradually beat in egg yolks and water. Place over hot water and cook, beating with a wire whisk, until mixture begins to thicken. When thick and smooth remove from heat.
2. Blend in lemon juice and cayenne pepper. Fold in tuna and parsley.
3. Heat oven to 400°F.
4. Spoon tuna filling in center of each crêpe. Roll up and placed folded side down in a shallow baking dish. Sprinkle with cheese.
5. Bake 10 to 15 minutes or until heated through.
6. Makes 6 servings.

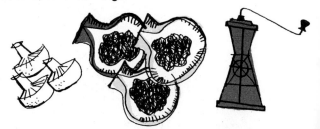

COQUILLES ST. JACQUES PARISIENNE

1 cup dry white wine
½ teaspoon salt
  Grind of fresh pepper
½ bay leaf
2 tablespoons minced shallots or green onions
1 pound sea scallops
½ pound fresh mushrooms, sliced
  Water
  Butter
4 tablespoons flour
¾ cup milk
2 egg yolks, beaten
½ cup heavy cream
¼ cup grated Swiss cheese

1. Combine wine, salt, pepper, bay leaf and shallots in a stainless steel or enameled saucepan. Bring to a boil and simmer 5 minutes.
2. Add scallops and mushrooms and enough water to just cover scallops. Bring to a boil. Cover, lower heat and simmer 5 minutes. Remove scallops and mushrooms and set aside.
3. Boil liquid down rapidly until it is reduced to 1 cup. Remove bay leaf.
4. Melt 3 tablespoons butter in a saucepan. Stir in flour. Remove from heat and slowly stir in the hot scallop liquid and the milk. Return to heat and cook, stirring constantly, until mixture boils and is smooth and thickened.
5. Beat together egg yolks and cream. Beat some of the hot sauce into egg yolks. Return to mixture in saucepan and cook over low heat, stirring constantly, for 1 minute. Season to taste with salt and pepper.
6. Cut scallops into small pieces. Fold into sauce with mushrooms. Butter scallop shells or small individual casseroles. Fill shells with scallop mixture. Sprinkle cheese over top of shells. Dot tops with 1 tablespoon of butter.
7. Preheat broiler.
8. Place on broiler rack and broil about 7 inches from source of heat until sauce is bubbly and the top is lightly browned.
9. Makes 4 to 6 servings.

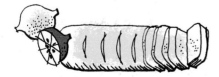

FISH SOUP-STEW

¼ cup olive oil, divided
1 large onion, chopped
3 cloves garlic, minced
1 leek, well cleaned and chopped
3 celery stalks, finely chopped
1 tablespoon leaf saffron
½ teaspoon thyme
1 bay leaf
1 can (1 pound 1 ounce) peeled Italian tomatoes with basil
1 large tomato, peeled and chopped
1 cup dry white wine
2 cups water
  Salt and pepper
1 teaspoon fennel seeds, crushed
2 pounds firm-fleshed fish (bass, carp or sea bass) cut into large serving pieces
2 dozen raw mussels, scrubbed and cleaned
2 dozen clams, washed
1 tablespoon anise liquer
¼ cup finely snipped parsley

1. Heat 2 tablespoons olive oil in a large heavy kettle. Add the onion, garlic, leek, celery and saffron. Cook, stirring, until limp but not browned.
2. Add thyme, bay leaf, tomatoes, wine, water, salt, pepper and fennel. Bring to a boil and simmer, uncovered, 45 minutes.
3. Add fish, mussels and clams. Cover. Bring to a high boil and cook 20 minutes. Season to taste with salt and pepper.
4. Stir in remaining olive oil, liqueur and parsley. Serve immediately with toasted French bread.
5. Makes 4 servings as a main dish.

Poultry

Pot-au-Feu freely translated means "Pot on the Fire" and is one of the best known French dishes. Pot-au-Feu is an easily assembled hearty stew-soup that simmers by itself for several hours. The simplicity of this famed dish comes as a surprise to the many people who think all French dishes are apt to be long and complicated.

Traditionally, a marmite or a large, tall straight-sided stock pot is used. Some people insist that it must be made of tinned copper, while others say that enameled cast iron or earthenware is the only kind of pot that gives the proper results. Actually, any large covered pot may be used, as long as it's reasonably heavy. Since it must accommodate a piece of beef, some sausage and a chicken, as well as an assortment of vegetables, it should measure 6 to 8 quarts. If you don't have a pot large enough, cook the meats and vegetables separately, using some of the stock from the meats for cooking the vegetables.

The service of this dish is a thing the French and the devotées of French cooking love to discuss. One group says that the broth created during the cooking is the only part worth eating, while those on the other side of the fence contend that it's the meat and vegetables that are worth waiting for. The best way to serve it is to have the bouillon for a first course and follow it with the meat and vegetables.

If you have any leftover bouillon, save it. This will provide the stock for many other good French dishes. It can be frozen and then used as needed.

POT-AU-FEU WITH ARTICHOKES

(shown opposite)

1½ pounds eye round of beef, tied
4 marrow bones
1 veal knuckle, split
1 carrot, coarsely chopped
1 onion, coarsely chopped
1 tablespoon salt
6 parsley sprigs
1 bay leaf
½ teaspoon thyme
4 cloves garlic
8 peppercorns
   Water
3½ pound chicken, cleaned and trussed
1 pound Polish sausage
6 medium carrots, peeled and halved
6 medium potatoes, peeled
6 medium artichokes
   Salt

1. In a very large pot combine beef, bones, knuckle, chopped carrot, onion and salt. Place parsley, bay leaf, thyme, garlic and peppercorns in a small piece of cheesecloth and tie it tightly. (This is called a bouquet garni.) Add to pot. Add enough water to cover. Bring to a boil slowly. Cover and simmer over low heat 1½ hours, skimming off foam occasionally.
2. Remove beef and bouquet garni. Set aside. Remove and discard bones and coarsely chopped vegetables from cooking liquid.
3. Return beef and bouquet garni to stock. Add chicken and sausage. Bring to a boil and simmer 15 minutes, skimming off foam occasionally.
4. Add carrots and potatoes. Cover and simmer about 45 minutes or until chicken and vegetables are tender.
5. While this is cooking, wash artichokes and cut in half. Cut off stem at base. Trim tips of leaves and cut off about 1 inch from tops of artichokes. Place artichokes in a separate pot. Add 2 to 3 inches of the stock in which meat is cooking. Cover and boil gently 30 to 40 minutes, or until base can be pierced easily with a fork.
6. Lift meats and vegetables from cooking stocks and arrange in serving dish. Combine stocks from meat and artichokes; skim off fat and season to taste with salt.
7. Serve stock in soup dishes as a first course. Serve meat and vegetables with mustard or horseradish, if desired.
8. Makes 6 servings.

POT-AU-FEU

3 pounds lean brisket of beef
¼ pound salt pork
1 onion stuck with 2 cloves
3 leeks, well washed and cut in chunks
1 stalk celery, cut in chunks
9 carrots, peeled and halved
1 turnip peeled and cut in chunks
   Sprig of parsley
1 teaspoon thyme
1 tablespoon salt
3½ pound chicken, cleaned and trussed
6 potatoes, peeled
1 small head cabbage, cut into 6 sections

1. In a very large pot put brisket, salt pork, onion stuck with cloves, leeks, celery, 6 carrot halves, turnip, parsley and thyme. Add enough water to cover. Bring to a boil over high heat. Add salt and cook gently over low heat for 1½ hours.
2. Add chicken and continue cooking 30 minutes.
3. Add potatoes, cabbage and remaining carrots. Continue cooking about 30 minutes or until chicken and vegetables are tender.
4. Serve the pot-au-feu in large soup plates, giving each person some broth, meat, vegetables and chicken. Serve with plenty of crusty French bread.
5. Makes 6 servings.

California Artichoke Advisory Board

CHICKEN AND GARLIC

⅓ cup olive oil or salad oil
4 stalks celery, cut into thin strips
6 sprigs parsley
1 teaspoon tarragon
2 whole clusters garlic
1 broiler-fryer, cut in quarters
  Salt
  Freshly ground black pepper
  Nutmeg
⅓ cup brandy

1. Heat oven to 375°F.
2. Pour olive oil into a casserole that has a very tightly fitting cover. Add celery, parsley and tarragon.
3. Separate garlic into cloves and peel. Cloves of garlic will peel easily if each one is placed on a board and pressed hard with the side of a knife or rapped smartly with the flat side of a cleaver. Do not smash garlic. Add garlic cloves to casserole.
4. Sprinkle chicken pieces with salt, pepper and nutmeg. Place chicken in casserole, turning each piece of chicken in the oil and vegetables. Add brandy.
5. Cover top of casserole with a piece of heavy-duty aluminum foil, pressing it down tightly on sides. Place lid on top.
6. Roast 1½ hours.
7. Open casserole just at serving time. Serve with slices of French bread fried in butter or oil, or pieces of toast. Spread garlic cloves and vegetables on each piece of bread or toast and cover with some of liquid in bottom of casserole.
8. Makes 4 servings.

CHICKEN MAXIMILIAN

2 broiler-fryer chickens, cut in quarters
1½ teaspoons salt
1 teaspoon paprika
¼ cup soft type margarine
2 tablespoons slivered orange rind
1½ cups orange juice
2 teaspoons instant minced onion
½ teaspoon ginger
½ teaspoon dried tarragon
4 teaspoons cornstarch
1 avocado

1. Sprinkle chicken quarters on both sides with salt and paprika.
2. Heat margarine in a large skillet over medium high heat. Add chicken quarters a few at a time and brown well on both sides.

Chicken takes on a fabulous taste when it is turned into Coq au Vin. Simmered to a turn with tiny onions, mushrooms and wine, it is delicious.

California Wine Institute

Remove chicken quarters as they get browned.
3. Return chicken to skillet. Add orange rind and juice, minced onion, ginger and tarragon. Cover and simmer, 20 to 25 minutes.
4. Remove chicken and place on a hot platter.
5. Blend cornstarch with a little cold water. Stir into sauce in skillet. Cook, stirring constantly, until mixture thickens and comes to a boil.
6. Peel and cut avocado in wedges. Arrange around chicken. Pour a little sauce on chicken and avocado. Serve remaining sauce with chicken.
7. Makes 8 servings.

COQ AU VIN

4 slices bacon
¼ cup butter or margarine
2 broiler-fryers, cut in quarters
16 small white onions
16 large mushrooms
2 cloves garlic, minced
1 bunch scallions, cleaned and cut up
¼ cup flour
3 cups dry red table wine
2 chicken bouillon cubes dissolved in
1 cup boiling water
2 teaspoons salt
¼ teaspoon pepper
½ teaspoon thyme
1 bay leaf

1. Cut bacon in small pieces. Place in Dutch oven over medium heat. Cook until bacon is crispy. Remove bacon pieces and reserve.
2. Place butter in Dutch oven with bacon fat. Brown chicken pieces well on all sides. Remove chicken pieces and reserve.
3. Peel onions, but leave whole. Clean mushrooms and leave whole. Place onions and mushrooms in hot drippings in Dutch oven and brown lightly. Remove onions and mushrooms.
4. Pour off drippings in pan, leaving about 2 tablespoonsful in pan. Add garlic and green onion. Cook over medium heat until onion is limp. Stir in flour and cook over medium heat about 2 minutes, stirring constantly, until flour is lightly browned. Remove from heat and stir in wine and chicken bouillon. Return to heat and cook, stirring, until mixture comes to a boil.
5. Season with salt, pepper and thyme. Add bay leaf. Add bacon bits, chicken pieces, onion and mushrooms. Cover tightly and simmer 30 to 45 minutes or until chicken is tender. Remove bay leaf.
6. Makes 8 servings.

BAKED CHICKEN CONTINENTALE

    2 broiler-fryer chickens, quartered
    2 teaspoons Ac'cent
 1½ teaspoons salt
    ½ cup margarine, softened
    1 clove garlic, crushed
    1 cup fine dry bread crumbs
    ½ cup grated Parmesan cheese
    ¼ cup chopped parsley
    1 teaspoon tarragon, thyme or rosemary
    ½ teaspoon dry mustard

1. Heat oven to 375°F.
2. Sprinkle chicken quarters on both sides with Ac'cent and salt. Combine softened margarine and garlic.
3. On a piece of waxed paper, combine remaining ingredients.
4. Spread chicken quarters on both sides with margarine-garlic mixture; dip in bread crumb mixture to coat well. Place in a baking pan.
5. Bake 1 hour or until chicken is tender.
6. Makes 8 servings.

TWIN CHICKENS ORANGE

    2 whole broiler-fryer chickens
    1 teaspoon salt, divided
    4 oranges
    3 sprigs of tarragon
    1 garlic clove, cut in half
    4 tablespoons sugar
    ¼ cup red wine vinegar
    2 cups chicken bouillon
    4 peppercorns
    1 tablespoon cornstarch

1. Heat oven to 375°F.
2. Sprinkle cavity of each chicken with ½ teaspoon salt. Hook wing tips into back.
3. Remove peel of 1 orange with a vegetable peeler, cutting peel into long strips. Reserve for sauce. Squeeze juice from this and 3 remaining oranges. Reserve juice for sauce. Cut 2 of the squeezed oranges into small chunks. Fill body cavities of chicken with orange sections and 1 sprig of tarragon each. Tie legs together with strings, then tie legs and tail together. Rub with garlic.
4. Place chickens in a shallow, open roasting pan. Roast 30 minutes per pound.
5. While chickens are cooking, prepare the sauce. Stir sugar and vinegar together in a saucepan. Bring to a boil, stirring until sugar is dissolved. Reduce heat and simmer about 5 minutes or until mixture thickens slightly. Add bouillon, remaining sprig of tarragon, peppercorns and salt to taste. Bring to a boil and simmer 10 minutes. Add orange juice. Add orange peel.

6. Pour sauce over chickens during the last half hour of roasting. Baste frequently.
7. Remove chickens to a heated serving platter. Remove cavity fillings and discard. Stir a little water into cornstarch. Stir mixture into orange sauce in pan. Bring mixture to a boil, stirring, until thick and clear.
8. Serve sauce with roast chicken.
9. Makes 8 servings.

POULET AU POT HENRI IV
(shown opposite)

    1 whole 3-pound broiler-fryer chicken
    2 cups water
 1½ teaspoons salt
    ½ teaspoon dried tarragon
    ½ teaspoon dried thyme
    2 sprigs parsley
    1 bay leaf
    6 peppercorns
    4 carrots, scraped and cut in 1½-inch pieces
    2 white turnips, pared and sliced
    4 leeks or 8 scallions, root and coarse green part removed, cut in 3-inch pieces

1. Place chicken in a large kettle. Add water, salt, tarragon, thyme, parsley, bay leaf and peppercorns. Bring to a boil. Reduce heat, cover and simmer 30 minutes.
2. Add carrots, turnips and leeks. Simmer, covered, another 30 minutes.
3. Remove chicken to a serving dish. Remove vegetables and place around chicken. Keep chicken and vegetables warm while making Lemon Sauce.
4. Makes 4 servings.

LEMON SAUCE

    1 tablespoon butter
    1 tablespoon flour
 1½ cups strained chicken stock from boiled chicken
    2 egg yolks
    ½ cup heavy cream
 1½ tablespoons lemon juice

1. Melt butter in a saucepan. Blend in flour.
2. Remove from heat and slowly stir in chicken stock, blending well.
3. Return to heat and cook, stirring constantly, until mixture comes to a boil.
4. Beat together egg yolks, cream and lemon juice. Pour a small amount of the hot mixture into egg mixture. Return to hot mixture in saucepan. Cook over low heat until sauce is thoroughly heated and slightly thickened.
5. Spoon a little sauce over chicken. Serve remainder in sauce dish.
6. Makes 2¼ cups sauce.

BAKED CHICKEN

¼ cup butter or margarine
1 broiler-fryer, cut in serving pieces
1 medium onion, chopped
½ pound fresh mushrooms, sliced
1 can (10 ounces) condensed cream of mushroom soup
¾ cup dry sherry
1 tablespoon chopped parsley
1 teaspoon salt
1 teaspoon paprika
Grind of fresh pepper
1 or 2 lemon slices

1. Heat oven to 350°F.
2. Melt butter in a large skillet over medium heat. Add chicken pieces and brown slowly on both sides. Remove from skillet and place in a shallow baking dish.
3. Add onions and mushrooms to butter in skillet and cook until limp, but not browned. Stir in soup, sherry, parsley, salt, paprika, pepper and lemon slices. Pour over chicken in casserole.
4. Bake 1 hour or until chicken is tender.
5. Makes 4 servings.

CHICKEN WITH EGGPLANT

1 broiler-fryer chicken, cut in serving pieces
Paprika
2 teaspoons salt, divided
¼ teaspoon pepper
2 tablespoons butter or margarine
½ cup chicken bouillon
1 clove garlic
1 medium eggplant, peeled and diced
4 scallions, cut in small pieces
2 tomatoes, peeled and diced
¼ teaspoon thyme
1 tablespoon parsley

1. Sprinkle chicken pieces with paprika and 1 teaspoon of the salt and pepper.
2. Melt butter in a large skillet over medium-high heat. Place chicken pieces in skillet, skin side down, and brown lightly on both sides. Remove chicken from skillet.
3. Add bouillon and simmer a few minutes, scraping brown particles from bottom of skillet. Return chicken to skillet. Add garlic, eggplant, scallions and tomatoes. Sprinkle with remaining salt, thyme and parsley. Cover and simmer 30 minutes or until chicken is tender.
4. Remove garlic clove before serving.
5. Makes 4 servings.

CHICKEN WATERZOIE

2 broiler-fryer chickens cut in serving pieces
1¾ cups water, divided
½ cup dry white table wine
1 bay leaf
1 onion, stuck with 2 cloves
1 stalk celery
1½ teaspoons salt
⅛ teaspoon pepper
⅛ teaspoon thyme
3 tablespoons flour
2 egg yolks
2 tablespoons lemon juice
1 teaspoon sugar
Parsley

1. Put chicken in a large pot. Add 1½ cups water, white wine, bay leaf, onion, celery, salt, pepper and thyme. Cover tightly and bring to a boil. Reduce heat and simmer 45 minutes to 1 hour or until chicken is tender.
2. Remove chicken and strain broth. Measure 2 cups of the broth into the pot. Combine remaining ¼ cup water and the flour to make a paste. Stir into broth in pot. Bring to a boil, stirring constantly.
3. Beat egg yolks, lemon juice and sugar together in a small bowl. Stir in a small amount of the hot mixture. Then gradually return to hot broth, stirring constantly. Heat but do not boil. Add chicken pieces and heat but do not boil.
4. Turn into serving dish and garnish with parsley.
5. Makes 8 servings.

CHICKEN TARRAGON

1 broiler-fryer, cut in serving pieces
1 tablespoon seasoned salt
½ teaspoon freshly ground black pepper
Dash of paprika
¼ cup butter or margarine
1 medium onion, thinly sliced
½ pound fresh mushrooms, sliced
1 teaspoon tarragon

1. Sprinkle chicken pieces with blended salt, pepper and paprika.
2. Melt butter in a large skillet over medium low heat. Add chicken pieces and brown slowly on all sides, 15 to 25 minutes. Remove chicken.
3. Add onions and mushrooms to skillet and cook until tender but not browned. Return chicken to skillet. Sprinkle with tarragon.
4. Cover tightly and simmer about 20 minutes, or until chicken is tender.
5. Makes 4 servings.

CHICKEN VÉRONIQUE

2 broiler-fryer chickens, cut in serving pieces
Salt
Paprika
½ cup butter or margarine, divided
1 onion, finely chopped
1 clove garlic, minced
¼ pound mushrooms, sliced
4 tablespoons flour
1 tablespoon sugar
2 cups chicken bouillon
2 tablespoons lemon juice
1 cup white seedless grapes

1. Sprinkle chicken pieces with salt and paprika.
2. Melt ¼ cup butter in skillet over medium heat. Add chicken and brown well on all sides. Remove chicken.
3. Add remaining ¼ cup butter to the skillet. Add onion and garlic and cook over low heat 5 minutes, stirring occasionally. Add mushrooms and cook 2 minutes.
4. Blend in flour and sugar. Add chicken bouillon and lemon juice. Cook, stirring constantly, until mixture comes to a boil and is thickened.
5. Add chicken pieces. Cover tightly. Lower heat and simmer 30 minutes or until chicken is tender. Add grapes the last 5 minutes.
6. Arrange chicken on a warmed serving platter and pour sauce over the top.
7. Makes 6 servings.

GINGER GLAZED CHICKEN

1 can (6 ounces) frozen orange juice concentrate, thawed, undiluted
¼ cup water
2 tablespoons soy sauce
¼ teaspoon pepper
1 teaspoon salt
1 garlic clove, crushed
2 tablespoons slivered candied ginger
1 broiler-fryer, cut in serving pieces

1. Combine orange juice, water, soy sauce, pepper, salt, garlic and candied ginger. Place chicken pieces in a shallow dish. Pour orange juice mixture over top. Let stand in refrigerator about 3 hours or overnight, turning occasionally.
2. Heat oven to 375°F.
3. Remove chicken from orange sauce and place in a baking pan. Bake about 45 minutes, brushing frequently with orange sauce mixture, until tender.
4. Heat remaining sauce and serve with chicken.
5. Makes 4 servings.

CHICKEN PILAF PROVENÇAL

4 tablespoons olive oil, divided
2 tablespoons butter
2 broiler-fryers, cut in serving pieces
1 tablespoon flour
2½ cups chicken broth or bouillon
1 teaspoon salt
30 cloves garlic, peeled
¾ cup long-grain rice

1. Heat 2 tablespoons olive oil and the butter in a heavy Dutch oven. Add chicken pieces and brown thoroughly on all sides. Remove chicken.
2. Stir in flour and blend. Slowly stir in chicken broth, salt and garlic cloves. Bring to a boil, stirring constantly.
3. Return chicken to Dutch oven. Lower heat, cover and simmer 45 minutes.
4. While chicken is cooking, fry rice in the remaining 2 tablespoons olive oil, until rice is opaque. When chicken has cooked 45 minutes, add rice, easing down into broth in Dutch oven. Cover and simmer 20 minutes longer.
5. Serve chicken and rice together.
6. Makes 6 servings.

POULET MASCOTTE

2 tablespoons olive oil
1 tablespoon butter
1 3-pound chicken, cut in serving pieces
12 tiny new potatoes, peeled
1 can (14 ounces) artichoke hearts, drained and cut into halves
1 teaspoon salt
¼ teaspoon white pepper
½ teaspoon crumbled thyme or rosemary
2 tablespoons snipped parsley

1. Heat olive oil and butter in a large skillet over medium high heat. When butter has stopped foaming, add chicken pieces and brown well on both sides. Remove chicken pieces.
2. Add potatoes and brown well on all sides. Remove potatoes.
3. Add artichoke hearts to skillet and brown on both sides.
4. Return chicken and potatoes to skillet with artichoke hearts. Add salt, pepper and thyme. Cover tightly and simmer over low heat about 20 minutes. Remove cover, increase heat slightly and cook 10 to 15 minutes or until chicken and potatoes are tender.
5. Remove chicken and vegetables to a warm serving platter and sprinkle parsley.
6. Makes 4 servings.

WINE-TARRAGON CHICKEN

    1 broiler fryer, cut in serving pieces
1¼ cups dry white wine, divided
    1 teaspoon dried tarragon
    ¼ cup butter or margarine
    ½ teaspoon salt
    ⅛ teaspoon pepper
    1 tablespoon flour

1. Arrange chicken pieces in a 9-inch square baking dish. Combine 1 cup wine and tarragon. Pour over chicken and refrigerate, covered, several hours or overnight.
2. Drain; reserving marinade. Pat chicken pieces dry with paper toweling.
3. Heat butter in a skillet over medium heat. Add chicken pieces and brown well on all sides. Remove chicken pieces as they brown. Pour off all but 2 tablespoons of the drippings in the skillet.
4. Return chicken to skillet. Sprinkle with salt and pepper. Add ¼ cup of the reserved marinade. Cover and simmer 25 to 30 minutes or until chicken is tender.
5. Combine flour with remaining ¼ cup white wine to make a smooth mixture.
6. Remove chicken to a heated serving platter. Pour remaining marinade into skillet. Add flour-wine mixture. Bring to a boil, stirring constantly. Reduce heat and simmer a few minutes longer. Pour sauce over chicken.
7. Makes 4 servings.

CHICKEN IN HERBS AND WHITE WINE

    2 whole chicken breasts
      Flour
    ½ cup butter or margarine
    ½ teaspoon salt
      Grind of fresh pepper
    1 tablespoon tarragon
    ¾ cup dry white wine, divided
    3 tablespoons snipped parsley

1. Have butcher split and bone chicken breasts. Place between 2 pieces of waxed paper and pound as flat as possible with a pounder or flat side of a heavy cleaver.
2. Dust breasts lightly with flour. Melt butter in a skillet over medium high heat. Add chicken breasts and brown lightly on both sides. Add salt, pepper, tarragon and ½ cup wine. Simmer breasts, uncovered, 5 or 10 minutes, or until tender. Place breasts on a warm serving platter.

3. Add parsley and remaining ¼ cup wine. Simmer over high heat, stirring, until sauce is reduced a little. Taste and add additional salt and pepper if necessary. Pour sauce over chicken breasts.
4. Makes 4 servings.

OVEN-BROWNED ROQUEFORT CHICKEN

    6 chicken pieces, breasts or whole legs
    3 tablespoons flour
1½ teaspoons salt, divided
    ¼ teaspoon freshly ground pepper
    1 teaspoon rosemary
    4 tablespoons butter or margarine
    ⅔ cup dairy sour cream
    2 teaspoons chopped chives
    ½ cup crumbled Roquefort cheese, packed
    2 teaspoons grated lemon rind
    2 tablespoons lemon juice
    ¼ cup slivered blanched almonds

1. Wipe chicken pieces with a damp paper towel. Combine flour, 1 teaspoon salt, pepper, and rosemary in a paper bag. Shake chicken pieces in flour mixture, coating each piece well.
2. Heat butter in a heavy skillet over medium heat. Brown chicken well on all sides. Remove to a shallow baking dish.
3. Heat oven to 350°F.
4. Blend together sour cream, remaining salt, chives, Roquefort cheese, lemon rind and juice. Spread mixture over chicken in baking dish.
5. Bake 30 minutes. Sprinkle almonds over top of chicken. Continue baking 10 to 15 minutes or until almonds are browned and chicken is tender.
6. Makes 6 servings.

CHICKEN BREASTS CHAUD-FROID
(shown opposite)

    3 large chicken breasts, split
      Water
    1 teaspoon salt
    1 stalk celery, with leaves, cut in 2-inch pieces
    1 carrot, cut in 2-inch pieces
    1 sprig parsley
    4 whole peppercorns
    2 tablespoons butter or margarine
    2 tablespoons flour
    2 cups chicken broth
    2 envelopes unflavored gelatine
    1 egg yolk
    ¼ cup cream
      Truffles or ripe olives

1. Place chicken breasts in a large saucepan. Add 2 cups water, salt, celery, carrot, parsley and peppercorns. Cover and simmer 30 minutes or until chicken breasts are tender. Remove chicken breasts and refrigerate until thoroughly chilled. Strain stock into another saucepan. Boil, uncovered, until stock is reduced to 2 cups.

2. Melt butter in a saucepan. Blend in flour. Remove from heat and gradually stir in reserved 2 cups of chicken broth. Cook, stirring constantly, until mixture thickens and comes to a boil. Simmer 5 minutes over very low heat.

3. Soften gelatine in cold water. Stir softened gelatine into hot mixture until dissolved. Remove from heat.

4. Beat egg yolk with cream. Blend a little of the hot sauce into egg yolk. Return mixture to hot sauce. Cook over low heat, stirring constantly, for 2 minutes. *Do not boil.* Remove from heat and chill until slightly thickened.

5. Remove skin from cold chicken breasts and place chicken on a cake rack over a shallow pan.

6. Spoon slightly thickened sauce over chicken breasts. If all of sauce runs off chicken, it is not thick enough and should be chilled a few more minutes. If sauce forms thick patches on chicken, it is too thick. This can be remedied by heating it slightly to thin it a little, then chilled again. Sauce will become firm quickly on the cold chicken.

7. Press pieces of truffles or olives into glaze to make flower or other design in center of each chicken breast. Place in refrigerator until ready to serve.

8. Makes 6 servings.

Famous French Cookery

CHICKEN BREASTS SUPREME

6 whole chicken breasts
2 teaspoons Ac'cent
  Salt and pepper
¾ cup butter or margarine, divided
¼ cup finely chopped onion
2 tablespoons finely chopped parsley
½ teaspoon rosemary
½ teaspoon basil
1½ cups packaged stuffing mix
½ cup boiling water

1. Heat oven to 350°F.
2. Cut chicken breasts in half and remove bones. Cut through thickest part of each half breast to form a pocket. Sprinkle with Ac'cent, salt and pepper.
3. Melt ½ cup butter in a saucepan. Add onion and cook until onion is tender but not brown. Remove from heat. Stir in herbs and stuffing mix. Add boiling water and mix well.
4. Fill pockets in chicken breast with stuffing mix. Secure with skewers.
5. Place chicken on a rack in a shallow baking pan. Melt remaining butter and brush over chicken breasts.
6. Bake about 1 hour or until chicken is tender.
7. Serve with Supreme Sauce.
8. Makes 12 servings.

SUPREME SAUCE

3 tablespoons butter or margarine
3 tablespoons flour
2 chicken bouillon cubes
1¾ cups boiling water
½ cup heavy cream
2 egg yolks
½ teaspoon paprika
2 teaspoons lemon juice
2 tablespoons finely chopped truffles, optional

1. Melt butter in a saucepan. Blend in flour and cook over medium heat 30 seconds. Remove from heat.
2. Add bouillon cubes to boiling water and stir until dissolved. Stir into flour-butter mixture.
3. Return to heat and cook, stirring constantly, until mixture thickens and comes to a boil.
4. Beat together heavy cream and egg yolks. Stir a small amount of the hot mixture into egg yolks and blend well. Return egg mixture to saucepan. Cook over low heat, stirring constantly, just until mixture comes to a boil. Do not boil.
5. Stir in paprika, lemon juice and truffles.
6. Serve with Chicken Breasts Supreme.
7. Makes about 2¼ cups sauce.

CHICKEN À LA VALLÉE D'AUGE

4 whole broiler-fryer chicken breasts
¼ cup butter or margarine
1 teaspoon salt
⅛ teaspoon pepper
⅓ cup Calvados or applejack
6 shallots or scallions, minced
1 tablespoon chopped parsley
¼ teaspoon dried thyme
¼ teaspoon rosemary
½ cup dry white table wine or apple cider
½ cup heavy cream

1. Cut chicken breasts in half and remove bones if desired. Melt butter in a large skillet over medium low heat. Add chicken breasts and cook until lightly browned, 15 to 20 minutes.
2. Add salt and pepper. Warm Calvados in a small saucepan and pour over chicken. Ignite with a match and allow Calvados to burn out.
3. Add shallots, parsley, thyme, rosemary and white wine. Cover tightly and simmer over low heat, 15 to 25 minutes or until chicken is tender.
4. Remove chicken breasts and place on a heated platter. Add heavy cream to sauce in pan and blend well. Stir and heat to serving temperature, but do not boil.
5. Sauce may be poured over chicken or served separately.
6. Makes 8 servings.

CHICKEN IN COGNAC-CREAM

2 whole chicken breasts
1 egg
  Water
  Flour
  Fine dry bread crumbs
  Salt
  Pepper
6 tablespoons butter
3 tablespoons warm cognac
1 cup cream
2 egg yolks, beaten

1. Have butcher split and bone chicken breasts. Place breasts between 2 pieces of

waxed paper and pound as flat as possible with the side of a heavy cleaver.

2. Beat egg with 1 tablespoon water in a flat dish. Dip flattened chicken breasts in flour, then in beaten egg and finally in bread crumbs. Sprinkle with salt and pepper. Chill breasts in refrigerator at least 2 hours.

3. Heat butter in a skillet over high heat to a point where it is bubbling, but not smoking. Brown chicken breasts quickly on both sides. Cook an additional minute or so on each side, or until tender. Carefully pour over warm cognac. Ignite with a match and allow to burn out. Remove chicken breasts to a warm serving platter.

4. Beat together cream and egg yolks. Reduce heat under skillet. Stir in cream and egg yolk mixture. Cook, stirring constantly, until mixture is slightly thickened. *Do not boil.* Taste and add salt and pepper if necessary. Pour sauce over chicken.

5. Makes 4 servings.

CHICKEN BREASTS ARGENTEUIL

   4 whole chicken breasts
   Soft type margarine
   Salt
   Pepper
   Tarragon
   2 packages (10 ounces each) frozen
     asparagus, defrosted
   3 egg yolks
   2 tablespoons lemon juice
   ¼ teaspoon dry mustard

1. Heat oven to 375°F.
2. Have butcher bone and remove skins from each chicken breast. Cut each breast in half. Place each half between 2 pieces of aluminum foil and pound with the flat side of cleaver or rolling pin. Spread inside of each chicken breast with margarine and sprinkle lightly with salt, pepper and tarragon. Place 3 or 4 asparagus spears crosswise in center of each breast and fold ends over. Fasten with skewer or wooden picks. Place fold side down in a shallow baking pan. Spread tops of chicken breasts with margarine.
3. Bake 45 minutes, or until chicken is tender and lightly browned.
4. When chicken is almost done, combine egg yolks, lemon juice, ¼ teaspoon salt and dry mustard in the top of a double boiler. Add ½ cup soft type margarine. Place over hot,

not boiling, water and cook, stirring with a wire whisk until sauce thickens. Remove from heat and serve over chicken breasts.

5. Makes 8 servings.

TURKEY-ALMOND CRÊPES

   1 cup plus 2 tablespoons sifted flour
   Pinch of salt
   3 eggs, beaten
   1½ cups milk
   1 tablespoon melted butter or margarine
   1½ tablespoons brandy
   Butter

1. Combine flour and salt in a bowl. Beat eggs and milk together. Stir into flour mixture and beat until smooth. This can be done on low speed of an electric mixer or with a wire wisk. Stir in melted butter and brandy. Let mixture stand for 2 hours before cooking.
2. Heat a small crêpe pan, 5½ to 6 inches in diameter across the bottom, over medium high heat.
3. When skillet is hot add ½ teaspoon butter and swirl around pan to cover sides and bottom. Pour in 1 full tablespoon batter. Rotate and tilt pan quickly to spread batter over bottom of skillet. This must be done before batter has a chance to set.
4. Cook crêpe about 1 minute or until it is set and browned lightly on the bottom. Loosen sides with a spatula and flip crêpe over quickly with the fingers. Brown lightly on second side. The second side will not brown as nicely as the first side, so it is usually turned inside when it is rolled around a filling.
5. Make crêpes and stack in a pile as they are baked. They may be used immediately or made early in the day and filled just before serving. They may also be frozen with a piece of waxed paper between each crêpe.
6. Fill with Turkey Almond Filling and proceed as in given recipe.
7. Makes 18 to 24 crêpes, depending on size.

TURKEY-ALMOND FILLING

4 tablespoons butter or margarine
4 tablespoons flour
2 cups turkey or chicken broth
1 teaspoon tarragon
1 teaspoon salt
2 tablespoons brandy
1 cup heavy cream
3 egg yolks
2½ to 3 cups turkey chunks
¾ cup toasted, salted almonds
½ cup grated Parmesan cheese

1. Melt butter in a saucepan. Stir in flour and cook 1 minute. Remove from heat and slowly stir in turkey broth, blending well. Return to heat and cook, stirring constantly, until smooth and thick. Stir in tarragon, salt and brandy.
2. Beat together cream and egg yolks. Stir a little of the hot sauce into the egg yolks, beating well. Return egg mixture to sauce in saucepan. Cook over medium heat, stirring constantly, about 2 minutes. *Do not boil.*
3. Combine half of the sauce with the turkey chunks. Keep warm.
4. Heat oven to 450°F.
5. Stir the almonds into turkey mixture. Divide mixture among crêpes and roll up. Place, fold side down, in a shallow baking dish. Combine remaining sauce with cheese. Pour over top of crêpes in pan.
6. Bake 5 to 10 minutes or until sauce is bubbly and mixture is browned on the top.
7. Makes 6 to 8 servings.

ORANGE DUCKLING AU VIN

6 whole oranges
⅔ cup port wine
2 ready-to-cook ducklings, 4½ to 5 pounds each
3 teaspoons salt
2 onions, sliced into rings
1¼ cups orange juice
1½ tablespoons sugar
1½ teaspoons lemon juice
⅔ cup chicken consommé

1. Heat oven to 475°F.
2. Peel 5 oranges and slice into thick cartwheel slices. Pour wine over slices and set aside.
3. Rinse ducks. Drain thoroughly and wipe dry inside and out with paper toweling. Rub cavities of each duck with salt. Cut remaining unpeeled orange into quarters. Place 2 quarters in each cavity. Remove fat from neck opening. Secure skin to back with skewer, cutting away extra skin. Cut away tail and most excess skin from cavity. Tie legs together. Fold wing tips back on the wings. Deeply prick entire surface of duck with a fork. Spread onion rings over bottom of a large shallow roasting pan. Place ducks, breast side up, on top. Roast 30 minutes. Reduce heat to 350°F. Remove ducks from pan. Drain off all fat. Place ducks on their sides and roast 25 minutes. Turn ducks on other side and roast 25 minutes. Return to breast-up position and roast about 30 minutes. Baste twice with ¾ cup of the orange juice during last 30 minutes of roasting.
4. While ducks are roasting, combine sugar and lemon juice in a large skillet. Cook over medium heat, stirring constantly, until mixture begins to caramelize and turns golden brown. Remove from heat. Immediately stir in ½ cup orange juice and consommé. Cook over high heat, stirring constantly, until caramel melts. Boil mixture about 5 minutes or until liquid is reduced to about ⅓ cup. Set aside.
5. Remove ducks from roasting pan, draining juice in cavities into roasting pan. Remove orange quarters from duck and discard. Strain drippings into a deep bowl. Return ducks to pan and place in oven, with the heat turned off, to keep warm.
6. Carefully skim all fat from drippings. Drain wine from orange slices and add wine and ¾ cup drippings to reserved caramel mixture in skillet. Boil briskly 5 minutes or until reduced to about ¾ cup.
7. To serve, cut ducks into quarters with duck shears or kitchen scissors. Cover each piece with a small amount of sauce. Serve each piece with a marinated orange section and remaining sauce.
8. Makes 8 servings.

POTTED DUCKLING

4½ to 5 pound duckling
Salt
Freshly ground black pepper
3 leeks
2 tablespoons flour
2 large carrots, peeled and sliced
2 white turnips, peeled and cubed
1 clove garlic, minced
½ cup dry white wine
1 cup canned, peeled tomatoes
½ cup frozen green peas
¼ cup chopped parsley

1. Heat oven to 500°F.
2. With poultry shears cut duck into 4 serving pieces. Cut away as much of the fat from around edges of duck as possible. Sprinkle with salt and pepper.
3. Heat a large skillet over high heat. Add duck pieces, fat side down, and cook quickly until well browned. Pour off fat from skillet. Turn duck over and brown other side.
4. Place duck in a heavy casserole. Add neck and gizzard. Bake, uncovered, 20 minutes. Pour off fat as it accumulates.
5. Clean leeks and split in half lengthwise. Rinse under cold running water to remove all sand. Shake out moisture and cut in pieces, all except the very top tough part of leek.
6. Place casserole on top of range over moderate heat. Let cook a few minutes. Add leeks. Sprinkle with flour and stir well. Add carrots, turnips and garlic. Add wine and tomatoes. Bring to a boil. Lower heat, cover tightly, and simmer about 40 minutes or until duck is tender. Add peas the last few minutes of cooking.
7. Sprinkle with parsley and serve.
8. Makes 4 servings.

WINE-GLAZED DUCK

1 duckling
Salt
Paprika
2 tablespoons grated onion
1 cup dry red wine, divided
⅓ cup brown sugar, firmly packed
⅓ cup granulated sugar
1 tablespoon cornstarch
¼ teaspoon salt
1 teaspoon grated orange peel

1. Have your butcher cut duckling into quarters. Trim off all excess fat.
2. Heat oven to 400°F.
3. Place duckling pieces in a shallow baking pan. Roast, uncovered, 30 minutes. Remove from oven and drain off all fat in the pan.
4. Season duckling with salt and paprika. Sprinkle with grated onion. Pour ¼ cup wine in bottom of the pan. Cover pan with a piece of aluminum foil. Continue roasting until duckling is tender, about 40 to 45 minutes.
5. Combine sugars, cornstarch, salt, orange peel and remaining ¾ cup wine in a saucepan. Cook over medium heat until mixture comes to a boil.
6. Remove duckling from oven. Pour wine

sauce over top of duckling. Roast, uncovered, about 10 minutes longer, or until duck is nicely glazed. Baste frequently with liquid in bottom of pan.
7. Makes 4 servings.

GAME BIRDS L'ORANGE

6 partridges or small game birds
Salt and Pepper
Salt pork or bacon
6 to 8 oranges
3 tablespoons butter or margarine
3 green onions, minced
¾ teaspoon dried tarragon
6 tablespoons currant jelly
¼ teaspoon dry mustard

1. Heat oven to 425°F.
2. With string, tie legs and wings close to body of each bird. Season with salt and pepper. Completely cover breast of each bird with slices of salt pork or bacon. Tie tightly in place with string. Place birds on a rack in a shallow, open roasting pan. Roast birds 30 minutes.
3. While birds are roasting prepare sauce. Wash oranges. With a vegetable peeler or a zester remove very thin orange colored top of the rind from one orange, shred into fine pieces with scissors to make 3 tablespoonsful of rind. Reserve.
4. Section 3 or 4 oranges to make about 1½ cups drained orange sections. To section, cut off peel in a circular motion, cutting deep enough to remove white membrane. Go over fruit again to remove any remaining white membrane. Cut along side of each dividing membrane from outside to middle of core. Remove section by section, over a bowl, to hold juice. Drain sections and measure juice. Squeeze juice from enough additional oranges to measure 1¼ cups orange juice. Reserve juice and sections.
5. In a large skillet melt butter over medium heat. Add onion and tarragon and cook about 4 minutes, stirring. Add orange juice, shredded peel, currant jelly, dry mustard and salt. Stir and bring to a boil.
6. Remove birds from oven. Remove strings and salt pork. Place birds in skillet. Cover tightly and simmer gently 15 to 20 minutes, turning birds occasionally.
7. Remove birds to a warm serving platter. Add orange sections to sauce. Heat quickly and serve with birds.
8. Makes 6 servings.

Meats

What is a cassoulet? It's a combination of beans and meats cooked in a rich broth in an earthenware utensil which at one time was known as the "Cassole d'issel".

There are various theories concerning a cassoulet and of course many variations. Some people would never make cassoulet without including preserved goose, others prefer duck. Some swear that the golden crust that forms on the surface must be broken several times during the baking and that this crust then becomes a part of the cassoulet. But no matter what the school of thought, it will usually contain pork, lamb, sausages and beans.

Here are 3 variations. Once you have tried these, you will probably want to go on and invent your own cassoulet.

WINE CASSOULET

1 pound white pea or navy beans
Water
½ pound salt pork, cut in slices
1½ pounds boneless lamb shoulder, cut in cubes
4 large pork chops
½ pound pork sausages
2 large onions, chopped
1 can (8 ounces) tomato sauce
½ cup dry red wine
3 cloves garlic, finely chopped
¼ cup chopped parsley
1 teaspoon thyme
1 bay leaf
Salt and pepper to taste

1. Wash and pick over beans, discarding hulls and imperfect beans. Put in a container and cover with water. Let stand overnight.
2. Drain beans. Place in a large saucepan and cover with cold water. Bring to a boil and then simmer slowly for about 1 hour, or until beans are tender. Drain beans and reserve liquid.
3. In a large skillet, fry salt pork until some of the fat has cooked out. Remove salt pork. Brown lamb, pork chops and sausages in pork fat. Drain thoroughly on paper towels.
4. Cut pork chops and salt pork into 1 inch pieces. Slice sausage.
5. Drain all but 2 tablespoons of the fat from skillet. Add onions and cook until onions are limp but not browned. Add tomato sauce, wine, garlic, parsley and seasonings. Combine tomato mixture with drained beans.
6. In a large casserole alternate layers of beans and meats, ending with a layer of beans. Pour reserved bean liquid over all ingredients, just enough to cover.
7. Heat oven to 350°F. Bake 1½ hours or until meats are tender.
8. Makes 8 servings.

QUICK CASSOULET

3 cans white beans
4 tablespoons salad oil
1 large onion, chopped
3 cloves garlic, minced
1 tablespoon chili sauce
½ teaspoon thyme
4 bacon slices, cut in pieces
3 lamb steaks
3 pork chops
1 pound Italian or garlic sausage
1 cup beef bouillon
½ cup dry bread crumbs

1. Heat oven to 350°F.
2. Drain beans and place in a large casserole.
3. Heat oil in a skillet. Add onion and garlic and cook until onion is tender but not browned. Add to beans with chili sauce and thyme.
4. Fry bacon in the skillet until almost done. Remove pieces of bacon and put in casserole. Brown lamb steaks and pork chops in bacon fat in skillet. Remove lamb and pork and cut meat in cubes. Add to bean mixture.
5. Prick sausage all over with a fork. Place in a skillet and cover with water. Bring to a boil and simmer 30 minutes. Remove and cut in slices. Add to bean mixture.
6. Toss bean mixture lightly. Pour beef bouillon over top.
7. Bake 30 minutes or until bubbly and piping hot. Sprinkle bread crumbs over top and bake an additional 5 minutes.
8. Makes about 6 to 8 servings.

Note: If you have leftover duck or goose, use in place of one of the meats.

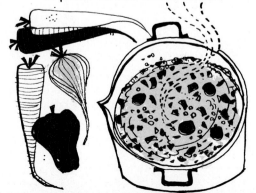

CLASSIC CASSOULET

5 cups white beans
4 ounces salt pork
1 bay leaf
3 sprigs parsley
1 teaspoon thyme
4 peppercorns
2 carrots, scraped and halved
1 whole onion
8 cloves
2 teaspoons salt
2 pound boned pork loin, cubed (keep the bones)
1½ pound boned shoulder lamb, cubed (keep the bones)
2 onions, chopped
2 cloves garlic, chopped
1 cup tomato purée
Beef bouillon
1 pound garlic sausage, either French style or hot Italian sausage
1 cup very fine bread crumbs, from crusty French bread if possible
Freshly ground black pepper

1. Pick over beans, discarding hulls and imperfect beans. Wash and place in a deep bowl. Add water to cover and let soak overnight.
2. Cover salt pork with water. Bring to a boil and simmer 5 minutes. Drain and dice.
3. Put beans in a Dutch oven or heavy heatproof casserole. Add enough water to cover. Add salt pork. Tie bay leaf, parsley thyme and peppercorns in a small piece of cheesecloth (bouquet garni). Add to beans with carrots, whole onion stuck with the cloves and salt.
4. Bring to a boil. Reduce heat, cover, and simmer gently about 1 to 1½ hours or until beans are just tender. Do not overcook. Remove bouquet garni, carrots and onion.
5. While beans are cooking prepare meat. Brown the pork and lamb cubes and bones in a large skillet or Dutch oven. Add chopped onions and garlic and cook 2 minutes. Stir in tomato purée. Cover and simmer about 1 hour, or until meat is tender. During cooking time, add beef bouillon as needed.
6. Prick sausage all over with a fork. Place in a skillet and cover with water. Bring to a boil and simmer 1 hour. Drain and cut in slices about ½ inch thick.
7. When meat is done, remove bones. Combine meat mixture with cooked beans. Taste and add salt and pepper if necessary. Add more beef bouillon if mixture is too dry.
8. Preheat oven to 375°F.
9. In a deep casserole place layers of the bean and meat mixture with slices of sausage between. Top layers with sausage slices. Combine bread crumbs with a good grind of pepper. Sprinkle over top.
10. Bake 1 to 1½ hours. As bread crust bakes and dries out on top of casserole, push it gently down into the casserole. When casserole is bubbling hot, it is ready to serve.
11. Makes about 12 servings.

CHOUCROUTE GARNIE

3 pounds sauerkraut
½ pound salt pork, sliced
1 large onion, thinly sliced
1 large Polish or Italian sausage, cut into 2-inch pieces
1 pound smoked loin of pork
1 bay leaf
¼ teaspoon thyme
1 teaspoon freshly ground black pepper
6 juniper berries, optional
2 cups dry white wine or beer
2 cups water
12 medium potatoes, peeled and boiled
12 frankfurters

1. Place sauerkraut in a deep bowl. Fill bowl with cold water and let stand a few minutes. Drain off water. Wash sauerkraut in bowl in more running water. Drain and squeeze out as much water as possible. Set aside.
2. Brown salt pork pieces in a large Dutch oven. When pork is browned and there is some fat in bottom of Dutch oven, add the onion, sausage and loin of pork. Brown meat and sausage on all sides. Remove meat and reserve.
3. Add sauerkraut to pan with bay leaf, thyme, pepper and juniper berries. Add wine or beer and water. Cover pan and simmer about 3 hours, stirring occasionally. Add more liquid, if necessary, to keep top of sauerkraut covered.
4. Return sausage and pork to Dutch oven. Cover tightly and simmer about 45 minutes.
5. Add potatoes and frankfurters. Cover and simmer about 15 minutes or just until potatoes and frankfurters are heated through.
6. To serve: Place sauerkraut in center of a large heated platter. Cut pork into thin slices and arrange on sauerkraut. Surround with sausage, potatoes and frankfurters.
7. Serve with a variety of mustards and either dry white wine or beer.
8. Makes 6 to 8 servings.

ROAST FRESH HAM

1 fresh ham, 6 to 8 pounds, boned and tied
1 bottle dry red wine
2 to 3 cloves garlic, crushed
1 onion, thinly sliced
1 bay leaf
½ teaspoon ground cloves
¼ teaspoon ground ginger
¼ teaspoon nutmeg
1 tablespoon salt
1 teaspoon crushed rosemary
½ cup golden raisins
½ cup pine nuts
   Tabasco

1. Place meat in a deep bowl or earthenware casserole. Combine remaining ingredients and pour over ham. Cover and let stand in refrigerator 3 days, turn occasionally.
2. On the day ham is to be cooked, remove from refrigerator and let stand in marinade at room temperature for several hours.
3. Heat oven to 325°F.
4. Remove ham from marinade and pat dry with paper toweling. Place on a rack in a shallow roasting pan. Insert meat thermometer in thickest part of ham.
5. Roast 25 to 30 minutes per pound of meat, or until a meat thermometer registers well done. Baste frequently with the marinade during cooking time.
6. Remove ham to a heated serving platter.
7. Skim fat from hot marinade. Strain into a saucepan. If sauce has cooked down too much, add a little more red wine. Season to taste with salt and pepper. Add raisins, pine nuts and a dash of Tabasco. Serve with sliced ham.

SAUSAGE IN WINE

1½ pounds pork sausage
¼ cup water
¾ cup dry white wine
1 tablespoon butter
1 tablespoon flour
1 cup beef bouillon
1 egg yolk, beaten
1 tablespoon lemon juice

1. Place sausage in a large skillet. Add water. Cover and simmer 5 minutes. Drain off water and continue cooking 10 minutes or until sausage is well browned on all sides.
2. Pour fat off skillet. Add wine and cook until wine is reduced to half the original volume.
3. Meanwhile, melt butter in a small saucepan. Stir in flour. Stir in bouillon and cook, stirring constantly, until thickened.

4. Remove sausage to a heated serving dish and keep warm. Stir reduced wine into bouillon mixture. Stir a small amount of the hot mixture into beaten egg yolk. Return mixture to saucepan. Stir in lemon juice. Cook over very low heat, stirring constantly, for 1 minute. Taste and season.
5. Pour sauce over sausage and serve.
6. Makes 4 servings.

PORK CHOPS IN VERMOUTH

¼ cup flour
1 teaspoon salt
½ teaspoon thyme
¼ teaspoon pepper
6 pork chops, cut ½ inch thick
2 tablespoons butter
2 tablespoons salad oil
½ cup dry vermouth or dry white wine

1. Combine flour, salt, thyme and pepper. Cut as much fat from pork chops as possible. Dust pork chops with flour mixture.
2. Heat butter and oil in a heavy skillet over medium heat. Add pork chops and cook until golden brown on both sides. Drain off every bit of fat from the skillet. Add vermouth. Cover and simmer about 30 minutes or until pork chops are tender.
3. Add more wine during cooking time, if necessary, to keep chops from sticking.
4. Makes 6 servings.

PORK CHOPS AND OLIVES MARSALA

¼ cup flour
1 teaspoon salt
¼ teaspoon pepper
4 shoulder pork chops, about ¾ inch thick
1 clove garlic, halved
3 tablespoons salad oil
½ cup water
½ cup marsala wine
½ cup sliced pimiento-stuffed olives
2 tablespoons chopped parsley

1. Combine flour, salt and pepper. Rub pork chops with garlic and dredge in flour.
2. Heat oil in a skillet. Brown pork chops well on both sides. Drain off excess fat.
3. Pour water over meat. Reduce heat. Cover tightly and simmer 30 minutes.
4. Add wine and olives and continue cooking 30 minutes or until chops are tender.
5. Sprinkle parsley on top just before serving.
6. Makes 4 servings.

PAUPIETTES AU PÂTÉ

8 veal scallops
Salt
Freshly ground black pepper
1 can (4½ ounces) smoked liver pâté, chilled
¼ cup butter or margarine
2 tablespoons brandy
1 clove garlic, chopped
1 onion, chopped
½ cup dry white wine
2 tablespoons snipped parsley

1. Place veal slices between 2 pieces of aluminum foil. Pound until very thin with a pounder or the flat side of a cleaver. Sprinkle with salt and pepper.
2. Open can and remove pâté carefully. Cut pâté into 8 equal sized strips. Place strips of pâté on slices of veal. Roll veal around pate. Tie rolls with string.
3. Melt butter in a skillet. When foam subsides, add veal and cook gently until golden brown on all sides.
4. Warm brandy. Pour over veal and ignite with a match. Allow flames to burn out. Add garlic, onion and wine. Cover and simmer over low heat about 30 minutes or until veal rolls are tender.
5. Remove veal rolls to serving platter, scrape up juices in bottom of pan and pour over veal.
6. Serve with mushrooms, artichoke hearts and canned French petit pois.
7. Makes 6 to 8 servings.

◀ SHERRIED SWEETBREADS AND HAM (shown opposite)

2 quarts water
2 tablespoons lemon juice
2 tablespoons salt
3 pairs veal sweetbreads, about 3 pounds
4 tablespoons butter
1 green pepper, sliced
1 large onion, minced
¼ cup flour
¼ teaspoon pepper
1 cup non-dairy powdered cream
2 cups boiling chicken broth or bouillon
¼ cup sherry
6 slices cooked ham, heated
Buttered toast points

1. In a large kettle combine water, lemon juice and salt. Bring to a boil. Add sweetbreads, reduce heat and simmer 20 minutes. Drain and plunge in cold water. Let stand a few minutes. Hold sweetbreads under cold water and remove membrane and veins. Cut sweetbreads into bite-sized pieces.
2. Melt butter in a heavy saucepan over medium heat. Add green pepper and onion; cook until tender and very lightly browned. Blend in flour and pepper.
3. Remove from heat. Add powdered cream and then boiling chicken broth. Beat with a wire whisk to blend. Cook over moderately high heat, stirring constantly, until mixture comes to a boil and is thickened. Stir in sweetbreads and sherry. Heat thoroughly.
4. Serve piping hot over slices of cooked ham. Garnish with buttered toast points.
5. Makes 6 servings.

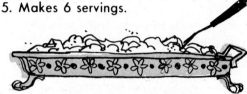

VEAL ITALIENNE

8 very thin veal cutlets
4 thin slices Gruyère or Swiss cheese
4 thin slices prosciutto
Salt
Freshly ground black pepper
Flour
2 tablespoons butter
3 tablespoons olive oil
½ cup dry white wine
½ cup chicken bouillon

1. Have butcher flatten veal until it is ⅛ to ¹⁄₁₆ inch thick.
2. Place a slice of cheese and a slice of prosciutto on 4 pieces of veal. Top with remaining 4 slices of veal. Press edges of veal together to seal, or fasten securely with toothpicks.
3. Season with salt and pepper. Dip in flour and shake off excess flour.
4. Melt butter and oil in a skillet over medium high heat. When the foam subsides, add veal and cook, two at a time, turning gently, until well browned on both sides. Remove veal to a heated platter.
5. Discard most of fat from skillet, leaving a thin film on the bottom. Pour in wine and bouillon and bring to a boil, stirring up any browned bits of veal on bottom of pan.
6. Return veal to pan. Reduce heat, cover tightly and simmer about 20 minutes, or until veal is tender. Turn veal over once during cooking period.
7. Remove veal to a heated serving platter and pour sauce over the top.
8. Makes 4 servings.

VEAL SCALLOPS MARSALA

1½ pounds veal scallops
   Flour
3 tablespoons butter or margarine
3 tablespoons salad oil
   Salt and pepper
   Marsala wine
¼ cup chopped parsley

1. Ask butcher to pound scallops paper thin. If butcher does not pound them thin enough, do it at home. Place each scallop between 2 pieces of waxed paper and pound with the flat side of a cleaver, a meat pounder or any heavy flat object.
2. Dust scallops with flour. Melt butter in large skillet, add oil and heat. Brown scallops quickly.
3. Cover with Marsala and continue cooking until the wine is reduced to half. Turn scallops once during cooking.
4. When wine is reduced and the meat is tender, remove meat to hot platter and add ¼ cup Marsala to the pan.
5. Bring to a boil, add parsley and pour over the veal.
6. Serve with hot cooked rice, if desired.
7. Makes 4 servings.

CÔTÉ DE VEAU QUERCYNOISE

6 to 8 veal chops, about 1 inch thick
   Salt and pepper
¼ cup butter
¼ cup olive oil
1½ cups chicken broth
1 clove garlic, minced
1 can (5 to 10 ounces) cèpes or chanterelles, (wild French mushrooms)

1. Roll ends of chops. Fasten ends with skewers. Sprinkle both sides of the chops with salt and pepper.
2. Heat butter and olive oil in a skillet over medium heat until foam begins to subside. Add chops and cook until golden brown on both sides. Continue cooking until chops are cooked to the desired degree of doneness. Remove chops to a hot platter and keep warm.
3. Add chicken broth and garlic to pan drippings, stir to remove browned bits from bottom of pan.
4. Wash mushrooms under running water. Drain and blot dry. Slice. Add mushrooms to sauce and cook briskly for 5 minutes. Pour mixture over chops. Serve immediately.
5. Makes 6 to 8 servings.

VEAL SCALLOPS JARNAC

12 veal scallops
   Flour
6 tablespoons butter
2 tablespoons salad oil
½ teaspoon salt
½ teaspoon freshly ground pepper
1 teaspoon tarragon
3 tablespoons warm cognac
¾ cup heavy cream
2 egg yolks, beaten

1. Sprinkle the veal scallops very lightly with flour.
2. Heat butter and salad oil in a skillet over high heat. Quickly cook the veal, turning several times, until browned on both sides. Reduce heat and add the salt, pepper and tarragon.
3. Pour the warm cognac over top of veal. Ignite with a match and allow flames to burn out. Remove scallops to a platter.
4. Beat together the cream and egg yolks. Reduce heat under skillet to very low. Add cream mixture to skillet and cook, stirring constantly, until mixture begins to thicken. Serve sauce with the veal scallops.
5. Makes 6 servings.

VEAL ROULADES

18 veal scallops
   pound ground ham
3 cloves garlic crushed
3 tablespoons snipped parsley
1 teaspoon rosemary
   Sprinkle of nutmeg
   Salt and pepper
6 strips of bacon
   Salad oil
⅔ cup white wine
1 bay leaf

1. Place veal between 2 pieces of waxed paper. Pound with a pounder or the flat side of a heavy cleaver.
2. Combine ham, garlic, parsley, rosemary, nutmeg and salt and pepper to taste. Divide this mixture evenly on top of each veal slice. Roll up and tie firmly with heavy string.
3. Cut bacon strips in pieces. Cook in heavy skillet until bacon is crisp and fat is rendered out. Remove bits of bacon. Brown veal rolls in hot bacon fat on all sides. Add salad oil, if needed, during browning time.
4. Add wine, bay leaf and bacon bits. Cover tightly and simmer over low heat 1 hour or until veal is tender.
5. Remove string before serving. Serve with sauce over each roulade.
6. Makes 6 to 8 servings.

VEAL CHOPS WITH MUSHROOMS

    4 loin veal chops, about 1¼ inches thick
    ⅓ cup butter or margarine
    ½ pound mushrooms, sliced
    2 tablespoons lemon juice
    ½ cup sliced onion
    ½ clove garlic, crushed
    ¼ cup flour
    1 teaspoon salt
    ⅛ teaspoon freshly ground pepper
    1 can (10½ ounces) condensed beef
      bouillon
    ⅔ cup dry white wine
    1 teaspoon chopped fresh tarragon leaves
    ½ teaspoon snipped chives

1. Trim excess fat from chops. Roll up ends of chops and fasten with wooden picks.
2. Melt butter in a skillet over medium high heat. Brown chops on both sides. Remove chops and set aside.
3. Sprinkle mushroom slices with lemon juice. Place in the skillet with onion and garlic. Cook, stirring, until golden, about 5 minutes. Remove mushrooms and onions and set aside.
4. Stir flour, salt and pepper into drippings in the skillet. Gradually stir in bouillon and wine. Add tarragon and chives. Bring to a boil, stirring constantly.
5. Add chops and cooked vegetables. Cover and simmer over low heat 30 minutes or until chops are tender.
6. To serve, remove chops to a heated serving platter. Remove picks from chops. Serve with gravy and vegetables.
7. Makes 4 servings.

VEAL CHOPS

    6 veal chops, cut ½ inch thick
      Flour
    ¼ cup salad oil
    ¼ cup butter or margarine
    6 cloves garlic
    2 medium bay leaves
    ½ teaspoon thyme
      Salt and pepper
    2 tablespoons red wine vinegar
    ½ cup chicken bouillon
    ¼ cup water

1. Dredge chops lightly on all sides with flour. Heat oil and butter in a skillet large enough to hold all the chops. Brown chops lightly on both sides.
2. Scatter garlic cloves around chops. Place a piece of bay leaf on top of each chop. Add thyme, salt and pepper. Cover tightly

and simmer chops 30 minutes or until tender and the sauce in skillet is syrupy. Remove chops to a hot serving platter and keep warm.
3. Stir vinegar into skillet and cook over high heat until it has evaporated. Stir in bouillon and water and simmer, stirring, about 5 minutes. Taste and add salt and pepper if desired. Pour sauce over chops.
4. Makes 6 servings.

VEAL MARENGO

    2 pounds boneless shoulder of veal
    1½ tablespoons olive oil
    1 clove garlic, minced
    10 small white onions, peeled
    ½ pound mushrooms, sliced
    1¼ teaspoons salt
    ¼ teaspoon freshly ground black pepper
    1½ tablespoons flour
    1 can (8 ounces) tomato sauce
    ½ cup dry white wine
    1 cup canned chicken broth
      Bouquet garni

1. Cut veal into 1½-inch cubes. Heat olive oil in a skillet with the garlic. Brown veal in hot oil, cooking only enough pieces at a time to cover the bottom of skillet. Remove veal and place in a casserole.
2. Brown onions in hot olive oil in skillet. Remove onions and place over veal.
3. Add mushrooms and brown lightly and quickly. Remove mushrooms and place over top of veal.
4. Stir salt, pepper and flour into remaining oil in skillet. Add tomato sauce, wine and broth. Cook, stirring constantly, until smooth and slightly thickened. Pour over veal in casserole.
5. Add the bouquet garni consisting of a small stalk of celery with leaves, 2 sprigs of parsley a bay leaf and a bit of thyme. Tie together with stem of the parsley or tie up in a small piece of cheesecloth.
6. Heat oven to 325°F.
7. Cover casserole with a lid or heavy duty aluminum foil. Bake 1¼ hours or until veal is tender.
8. Remove bouquet garni and discard.
9. Makes 6 servings.

VEAL IN CREAM

½ cup butter or margarine, divided
1 onion, chopped
2 cloves garlic, minced
2 pounds boneless veal shoulder, cut in
   1½-inch cubes
2 cups strong chicken bouillon
1 teaspoon salt
   Freshly ground black pepper
1½ cups heavy cream
1 pound mushrooms, cut in halves
¼ cup cognac

1. Melt ¼ cup butter in a heavy skillet. Add onion and garlic and cook until limp but not browned.
2. Add veal and cook, stirring until veal loses its pink color. Do not brown. Add bouillon, salt and pepper. Cover and simmer gently 1½ hours.
3. Add cream and simmer uncovered about 30 minutes. Stir occasionally.
4. Melt remaining butter in a skillet. Add mushrooms and cook about 3 minutes. Add mushrooms to veal mixture and simmer 15 minutes longer.
5. Stir in cognac and heat before serving.
6. Makes 6 servings.

BRAISED SHOULDER OF VEAL

4 pounds veal shoulder
2 cloves garlic
4 tablespoons butter
1 teaspoon salt
1 teaspoon freshly ground pepper
1 cup bouillon
1 cup dry white wine
1 teaspoon tarragon
1 onion
½ bay leaf

1. Have butcher bone, roll and tie veal shoulder. Be sure to take the bones also.
2. Make small incisions in the meat with a sharp knife and insert thin slivers of garlic.
3. Melt butter in Dutch oven over medium high heat. Add veal and brown well on all sides, turning often.
4. Sprinkle with salt and pepper. Add bouillon, white wine, tarragon, onion and bay leaf. Add the veal bones.
5. Cover and simmer gently about 2 hours or until veal is tender.
6. Remove veal to a hot serving platter. Remove strings and slice. Skim fat from juices in the pan. Remove onion, bay leaf and bones. Serve sauce with veal.
7. Makes 4 to 6 servings.

BLANQUETTE DE VEAU

1½ pound shoulder of veal
1 quart water
1 tablespoon salt
⅛ teaspoon powdered thyme
1 bay leaf
1 sprig parsley
12 small white onions
6 carrots, scraped and quartered
2 tablespoons butter or margarine
2 tablespoons flour
2 tablespoons lemon juice
2 egg yolks
½ teaspoon Tabasco
   Chopped parsley

1. Have veal cut into 1¼-inch cubes. Put in a deep saucepan with water, salt, thyme, bay leaf and parsley. Cover and simmer 1 hour, or until meat is almost tender.
2. Add onions and carrots and continue cooking until meat and vegetables are tender. Drain off stock and add enough water to make 2 cups liquid.
3. Melt butter in a saucepan. Stir in flour. Slowly stir in hot stock from veal. Cook, stirring constantly, until thickened.
4. Combine lemon juice and slightly beaten egg yolks. Stir about 1 cup of the hot sauce slowly into egg yolk mixture. Return to remaining sauce in saucepan. Cook over low heat until slightly thickened, *do not boil.* Stir in Tabasco.
5. Add sauce to veal and vegetables and heat but do not boil.
6. Arrange on a heated serving dish. Sprinkle with parsley. Serve with cooked rice or noodles.
7. Makes 6 servings.

SAUTÉED CALVES' LIVER

4 slices calves' liver, cut ⅜-inch thick
   Salt and pepper
¼ cup flour
2 tablespoons butter
2 tablespoons salad oil

1. Have butcher remove filament from slices of liver.
2. Sprinkle with salt and pepper. Dredge with flour and shake off excess flour.
3. Heat butter and oil in skillet until butter foam subsides and it just begins to turn brown. Place liver in skillet and cook 2 to 3 minutes. Turn liver and cook 2 to 3 minutes on second side.
4. Liver is done when its juices run a very pale pink when slice is pricked with a fork.
5. Makes 4 servings.

VEAL KIDNEYS IN RED WINE

  4 veal kidneys
 10 mushrooms
  4 tablespoons butter
  4 green onions, cleaned and chopped
    Salt and pepper
 ½ cup red wine

1. Slice kidneys in thin slices and remove hard core and excess fat.
2. Clean and slice mushrooms.
3. Melt butter in a heavy skillet over medium high heat. Add kidney and cook quickly until nicely browned on both sides.
4. Add mushrooms and green onions and cook about 5 minutes, stirring.
5. Sprinkle with salt and pepper and add red wine. Cook 4 to 5 minutes or until kidneys are tender and ingredients blended. Taste and add more seasoning if necessary.
6. Serve on buttered toast or fried bread.
7. Makes 4 to 6 servings.

KIDNEY AND MUSHROOM SAUTÉ

  6 veal kidneys
  6 tablespoons butter
 ½ pound small whole mushrooms
  6 tablespoons flour
  1 cup non-dairy powdered cream
  2 cups hot beef broth
 ¼ cup sherry
    Salt and pepper to taste

1. Trim kidneys by removing fat and the thin filament surrounding kidneys. Cut into slices.
2. Melt butter in a skillet over very high heat. When foam from butter subsides a little, add kidneys and cook very quickly, about 3 minutes. Remove kidneys to a chafing dish or casserole. Reduce heat a little and cook mushrooms until lightly browned on all sides. Remove to chafing dish.
3. Add flour to liquid in skillet, blending with a wire whisk; cook and stir 1 minute, but do not brown.
4. Remove from heat and stir in cream and hot beef broth all at once. Beat with wire whisk to blend.
5. Cook over moderately high heat, stirring constantly, until sauce comes to a boil and thickens. Blend in sherry and seasonings.
6. Pour over kidneys and mushrooms and heat gently, but do not boil. Serve from chafiing dish or casserole.
7. Makes 8 servings.

LIVER JULIENNE

  1 pound calves' liver
    Flour
    Salt and pepper
    Paprika
  2 tablespoons olive oil
  2 tablespoons butter
  1 clove garlic, minced
 ½ cup dry white wine
  2 tablespoons snipped parsley
 ¾ cup dairy sour cream

1. Cut liver into thin strips about ½-inch thick. Dredge with flour seasoned with salt, pepper and a little paprika.
2. Heat oil and butter in a large skillet just until foam from butter begins to subside. Add strips of liver and garlic and cook very quickly, turning so that all the liver strips become browned and cooked. This should take about 2 to 4 minutes.
3. Remove liver to a hot platter and keep warm.
4. Pour off most of fat from skillet. Add wine and parsley and cook, stirring, so that brown bits are stirred up from bottom of pan. Add sour cream and heat but *do not boil.* Taste and add more seasoning if desired.
5. Return liver strips to pan and stir well. Serve with buttered noodles or hot cooked rice if desired.
6. Makes 4 servings.

CALVES' BRAINS BEURRE NOIR

  2 calves' brains
  1 teaspoon salt
  1 onion stuck with 1 clove
  1 bay leaf
    Pinch of thyme
  4 peppercorns
  2 tablespoons butter
  2 tablespoons vinegar

1. Soak brains in cold water for 2 hours. Remove thin outer skin as gently as possible, without tearing the flesh. Cover with cold water and soak for 3 hours. Drain.
2. Place brains in a large saucepan. Cover with cold water. Add salt, onion, bay leaf, thyme and peppercorns. Cover and bring to a boil. Lower heat and simmer 20 minutes. Set aside and keep warm.
3. In a small skillet melt butter and cook until butter is dark brown. Arrange brains on a heated serving dish and pour butter over.
4. Put vinegar in skillet and cook briskly. Pour over brains. Serve at once.
5. Makes 4 servings.

CALVES' BRAINS SAUTÉ

2 calves' brains
1 teaspoon salt
1 onion, stuck with 1 clove
1 bay leaf
   Pinch of thyme
4 peppercorns
2 tablespoons flour
¼ cup butter, divided
6 thin slices lemon
1 tablespoon snipped parsley

1. Soak brains in cold water for 2 hours. Remove thin outer skin as gently as possible without tearing the flesh. Cover with cold water and soak for 3 hours. Drain.
2. Place brains in a large saucepan. Cover with cold water. Add salt, onion, bay leaf, thyme and peppercorns. Cover and bring to a boil. Lower heat and simmer 20 minutes. Drain.
3. Cut brains into slices ½-inch thick. Dredge slices with flour.
4. Melt 2 tablespoons of the butter in a large skillet. Add brains and cook for 10 minutes or until well browned on both sides. Remove brains to heated serving dish and keep warm.
5. In a small skillet heat remaining butter until it is medium brown in color. Pour over brains. Serve with lemon slices and sprinkle with parsley.
6. Makes 4 servings.

VEAL CUTLETS À L'EVELYN

2 to 3 tablespoons salad oil
8 small veal cutlets, trimmed of tendons
   Salt and pepper
½ teaspoon paprika
1 scallion, cleaned and chopped
   Pinch of marjoram or oregano
2 tablespoons chopped onion
2 tablespoons chopped parsley, divided
1 clove garlic, crushed
   Water
½ cup cream
3 tablespoons brandy
2 to 3 tablespoons port, sherry or Madeira
2 egg yolks, well beaten

1. Heat oil in a large skillet over medium high heat. Sprinkle veal with salt, pepper and paprika. Sauté in oil until golden brown on both sides.
2. Add scallion, marjoram, onion, 1 table-spoon parsley and garlic. Cover and simmer about 10 minutes, or until veal is tender. Add a little water if mixture looks dry.
3. Remove veal to a warm serving plate.
4. Combine cream, brandy, port and well beaten egg yolks. Stir into skillet. Place over very low heat and cook, stirring constantly, until slightly thickened and heated through. Pour over veal and sprinkle with remaining tablespoon of parsley.
5. Makes 5 to 6 servings.

MOLDED VEAL

(shown opposite)

2 envelopes unflavored gelatine
1½ cups water
2 cans (10½ ounces each) condensed beef consommé
2 tablespoons lemon juice
1 jar (2 ounces) pimientos, sliced, drained
2½ cups cooked veal, cut into bite-sized pieces
¾ cup thinly sliced celery
1 jar (11 ounces) mixed pickles, drained
2 hard cooked eggs, sliced

1. Soften gelatine in ½ cup cold water. Heat remaining water with 1 can beef consomme. Add gelatine and stir until dissolved. Add lemon juice and remaining consomme.
2. Measure out ⅓ cup of the consommé mixture and put in electric blender. Add pimientos and blend until smooth. Pour into 1½-quart mold. Refrigerate until set.
3. Chill remaining consommé mixture until it mounds slightly when dropped from a spoon. Stir in veal, celery and ¾ cup of the pickles, chopped. Spoon into the mold on top of pimiento mixture. Chill until thoroughly set.
4. At serving time, unmold onto serving dish. Garnish with egg slices and remaining pickles.
5. Makes 8 to 10 servings as a first course, 6 servings as a main course.

National Biscuit Co.

Lamb

The French manner of roasting lamb differs from the American because our meat experts have found that lower oven temperatures result in less meat loss and juicier roasts. Hence, these recipes are "American style"—that is, roasted in a slow oven. However, if you wish to be truly French, prepare roast lamb as follows:

If you are fond of the flavor of garlic, make several incisions in the top of the lamb and insert a thin sliver of garlic in each incision. Put the meat in a very hot oven, 450° F., and sear for 15 minutes. Reduce heat to 350° F. and continue roasting until meat is of desired degree of doneness. For medium rare leg of lamb, it will take about 12 minutes per pound. For well done it will take about 15 minutes per pound.

ROAST LEG OF LAMB WITH SPICY WINE SAUCE

(shown opposite)

1 cup dry red wine
¼ cup salad oil
1 onion, coarsely chopped
2 cloves garlic, minced
½ teaspoon Tabasco
Salt
1 leg of lamb
Stewed Tomatoes

1. Combine wine, oil, onion, garlic, Tabasco and salt to taste. Place lamb in a glass or enameled-ware pan just large enough to hold it. Pour wine mixture over the top. Cover and let stand in the refrigerator 6 hours or overnight. Turn meat occasionally.
2. Heat oven to 325°F.
3. Remove lamb and pat dry with paper toweling. Place on a rack in a shallow roasting pan. Insert a meat thermometer into heavy part of leg, being careful not to touch the bone.
4. Roast meat about 25 minutes per pound or to the desired degree of doneness. Lamb should be pink in the center when it is eaten. Baste lamb occasionally with the wine marinade.
5. Serve with Stewed Tomatoes.
6. Makes 6 to 8 servings.

STEWED TOMATOES

2 tablespoons butter
2 cloves garlic, crushed
1 small onion, thinly sliced
2 cans (2 pounds 3 ounces each) plum tomatoes, drained and juice reserved
1 tablespoon sugar
1 teaspoon salt
Freshly ground pepper

1. Melt butter in a medium saucepan. Add garlic and onion and cook until limp but not browned.
2. Add reserved tomato juice and boil until reduced to 1⅔ cups.
3. Add tomatoes, sugar, salt and pepper to taste. Heat to serving temperature.
4. Makes 6 to 8 servings.

American Lamb Council

LEG OF LAMB IN PASTRY

3 lamb kidneys
Butter or margarine
Madeira
¼ pound mushrooms, cleaned and chopped
¾ teaspoon salt
½ teaspoon rosemary
¼ teaspoon thyme
¼ teaspoon tarragon
4 to 4½ pound leg of lamb, boned
1 package pie crust mix
1 egg yolk
2 tablespoons flour
1½ tablespoons red currant jelly

1. Remove fat and white veins from kidneys. Wash and pat dry with paper towels. Cut kidneys into tiny pieces.
2. Melt 3 tablespoons butter in a skillet over medium high heat. Add kidneys and cook until golden brown. Stir in 1 tablespoon Madeira, mushrooms, salt, rosemary, thyme and tarragon. Remove from heat and let stand.
3. Heat oven to 425°F.
4. Lay leg of lamb flat. Cut off most of the fat. Place kidney mixture in center of lamb. Roll up lamb and fasten with skewers or tie with string. Place on a rack in a shallow roasting pan. Rub the top with softened butter. Insert meat thermometer into thickest part of meat, not into the stuffing.
5. Roast about 60 minutes or until the meat thermometer registers 150°F.
6. Prepare pie crust mix, following directions on package. On a lightly floured board, roll pastry out into a 15- by 12-inch oval.
7. Remove roast from oven. Place roast in a clean, shallow roasting pan without a rack. Remove thermometer and skewers or cut off strings. Reserve first roasting pan.
8. Lay pastry over lamb in roasting pan. Press pastry against meat and tuck underneath to cover roast completely. Beat egg yolk with 1 teaspoon of water and brush over top of pastry.
9. Bake 15 to 20 minutes or until pastry is golden brown.
10. While meat is cooking, add 1 cup of water

Recipe continues on next page

to drippings in first roasting pan. Heat, stirring to loosen browned bits in bottom. Strain mixture and let stand a few minutes. Skim off as much fat as possible.

11. Melt 2 tablespoons butter in a small saucepan. Stir in flour and cook, stirring constantly, until slightly browned. Stir in strained drippings. Cook over medium heat, stirring constantly, until smooth and thickened. Stir in 3 tablespoons Madeira and red currant jelly. Heat thoroughly.

12. Remove lamb from roasting pan and place on carving board. Cut in slices and serve with gravy.

13. Makes 8 servings.

LEG OF LAMB WITH WHITE BEANS

1 pound dried pea beans
Water
¼ cup butter or margarine
2 cloves garlic
2 pounds onions, thinly sliced
Seasoned salt
½ teaspoon salt
¼ teaspoon freshly ground pepper
1 teaspoon rosemary, divided
2 cans (1 pound each) Italian plum tomatoes
1 leg of lamb, about 6½ to 7 pounds

1. Place beans in a large kettle. Cover with water. Bring to a boil over high heat and simmer 2 minutes. Remove from heat, cover and let stand about 1 hour.

2. Return beans to heat. Bring to a boil. Reduce heat and simmer covered about 1 hour or until beans are tender. Check liquid during cooking period, adding water if necessary. Drain beans.

3. Heat oven to 325°F.

4. Heat butter in a large skillet. Crush 1 clove of the garlic and add to hot butter. Add onions and cook until golden brown, stirring occasionally.

5. In the bottom of a shallow roasting pan combine cooked beans, onion mixture, 2 teaspoons seasoned salt, salt, pepper, ½ teaspoon rosemary and tomatoes. Blend thoroughly.

6. Split remaining clove of garlic and rub over entire surface of lamb. Sprinkle lamb with seasoned salt and remaining rosemary. Place lamb on top of beans. Insert a meat thermometer into heavy part of leg, being careful that it does not touch the bone.

7. Roast, uncovered, 3 to 3½ hours or until

meat thermometer registers medium well done.

8. Remove lamb to carving board. Turn beans into a serving dish. Serve slices of lamb with beans.

9. Makes 10 servings.

BRAISED STUFFED SHOULDER OF LAMB

(shown opposite)

5 pound boned and rolled lamb shoulder
3 tablespoons salad oil, divided
¼ cup finely chopped onion
12 saltine crackers, finely rolled
2 teaspoons grated lemon rind
1 teaspoon mint flakes, crushed
½ teaspoon salt
¼ teaspoon freshly ground black pepper
1 egg, slightly beaten
4 ounces boiled ham, cut in julienne strips
½ cup apple juice
1 can (10½ ounces) condensed beef consommé
2 cups cherry tomatoes
2 tablespoons flour
Cold water

1. Unroll meat, wipe with a damp cloth.

2. Heat 2 tablespoons oil in a Dutch oven. Add onion and cook until soft but not browned. Scrape onion and oil into a mixing bowl. Add crackers, lemon rind, mint flakes, salt and pepper. Add egg and blend lightly.

3. Spread stuffing mixture on meat. Spread ham strips out over top of stuffing. Roll up and tie securely.

4. Heat remaining tablespoon of oil in the Dutch oven. Brown lamb slowly on all sides. Add apple juice and half the can of consommé. Refrigerate remaining consommé for other use.

5. Heat oven to 325°F.

6. Cover Dutch oven and place in oven. Cook 2 to 2½ hours or until lamb is done. Add cherry tomatoes the last 10 minutes of cooking.

7. Transfer meat and tomatoes to a heated serving platter. Remove strings from meat and discard.

8. Blend flour with enough water to make a smooth paste. Add to meat juices in Dutch oven. Cook, stirring, until mixture comes to a boil. Simmer 2 minutes. Serve gravy with lamb.

9. Makes about 8 servings.

Beef Bourguignonne is probably one of the most famous of all French dishes. You can have it almost anywhere in the world and you can make the best one of all in your own home.

There are probably as many variations of Beef Bourguignonne as there are different ways of spelling its name. The meat may be cooked in one big piece, and then sliced for serving, or cut into cubes before cooking. Cut into cubes, it is tastier and generally preferred by most people.

Simply, it is beef cooked in red wine. The spices and herbs can vary, it can be cooked with or without vegetables, or in a number of combinations. It is best cooked in large quantities for a long period of time. Beef Bourguignonne is good the first day, but even better when reheated. It also takes well to the freezer, so freeze the leftovers and have them several weeks later.

BOEUF BOURGUIGNONNE

**5 pounds beef chuck or round, cut into
1½-inch pieces
1 tablespoon Ac'cent
1 tablespoon salt
¼ teaspoon pepper
½ pound salt pork
2 medium onions, chopped
1 clove garlic, minced
3 cups dry red wine
1 bay leaf
¼ cup chopped parsley
1 teaspoon thyme
1 pound mushrooms, cleaned and sliced
3 tablespoons flour**

1. Sprinkle beef with combined Ac'cent, salt and pepper.
2. Cut salt pork into small cubes. Heat an oven-proof casserole or Dutch oven over medium high heat. Add salt pork pieces and cook until golden brown. Remove pieces of salt pork. Add beef to hot fat, a few pieces at a time; brown well on all sides and remove.
3. Add onion and cook until onion is tender but not browned. Return salt pork and beef to Dutch oven. Add garlic, wine, bay leaf, parsley and thyme. Cover and simmer about 3 hours or until meat is tender. Add additional wine if necessary during cooking time.
4. Add mushrooms during the last 15 minutes of the cooking time.
5. Combine flour with a little cold water to make a smooth paste. Stir into hot mixture and cook, stirring constantly, until mixture is thickened.
6. Makes 12 servings.

OVEN-BAKED BEEF BOURGUIGNONNE

**4 pounds beef rump or beef chuck
⅓ cup warm cognac
2 whole onions, each stuck with 2 cloves
2 cloves garlic
1 teaspoon thyme
½ bay leaf
4 cups dry red wine
1 tablespoon salt
1 teaspoon freshly ground black pepper
1 slice orange
2 tablespoons butter
18 small white onions, peeled**

1. Have the beef rump tied. If there is very little fat on the outside, have the butcher tie on several pieces of beef suet.
2. Heat a Dutch oven over medium-high heat. Add beef and brown thoroughly on all sides. Pour warm cognac over beef and ignite with a match. Allow flames to burn out.
3. Heat oven to 300°F.
4. Add 2 cloved onions, garlic, thyme, bay leaf, dry red wine, salt, pepper and orange slice. Bring to a boil on top of the range.
5. Cover Dutch oven and bake about 2 hours. Turn once or twice during cooking period.
6. Melt butter in a skillet. Add white onions and brown on all sides. Add to beef in Dutch oven. Cook 30 minutes more or until beef is tender.
7. Remove beef and onions to a hot serving platter. Cook down liquid in Dutch oven. Strain and serve with slices of the beef.
8. Makes 8 to 10 servings.

 Beef Bourguignonne has become as much a part of our American cooking as of the French. It is a savory dish combining beef cubes, wine and herbs.
Ac'cent

POT ROAST PROVENÇAL

- 5 pounds eye round of beef, tied
- 12 to 14 whole pimiento-stuffed green olives
- 3 to 4 large cloves garlic, slivered
- 1 medium onion, sliced
- 1 stalk celery, cut into chunks
- 1 large bay leaf
- 4 whole cloves
- 1 tablespoon sugar
- 1 teaspoon Ac'cent
- ¼ teaspoon savory
- ¼ teaspoon peppercorns
- ¼ teaspoon salt
- 1½ cups dry red wine
- 2 tablespoons salad oil
- 1½ pounds peeled new potatoes
- 4 carrots, cut into 2-inch sticks
- 1 cup diced tomatoes
  Water
- 1 tablespoon flour

1. Stick a sharp pointed knife into the fat side of the meat, every inch or so, then wiggle it to make a hole. Put an olive and a sliver or two of garlic into each hole. Place meat in a large bowl. Add onion, celery, bay leaf, cloves, sugar, Ac'cent, savory, peppercorns, salt and any remaining garlic or olives. Pour wine over the beef. Let stand in the refrigerator overnight. Turn occasionally.
2. Remove beef and reserve marinade. Pat meat dry with paper toweling. Heat salad oil in a large Dutch oven. Add beef and brown slowly on all sides. Pour off any excess fat. Add marinade to beef. Cover tightly and simmer 3 to 3½ hours.
3. Add potatoes, carrots and tomatoes the last 30 minutes of cooking time. Cover and continue simmering until meat and vegetables are tender.
4. Remove meat to a hot serving platter. Remove vegetables with a slotted spoon and place around pot roast.
5. Strain liquid in pan and measure. Add enough water to make 2 cups. Return liquid to Dutch oven.
6. Blend flour with 2 tablespoons cold water. Stir into liquid and bring to a boil. Cook 1 minute, stirring constantly. Serve with beef.
7. Makes 6 to 8 servings.

Pot Roast Provencal may well become a favorite in your home. Made with garlic, herbs and wine, it has the extra added fillip of stuffed green olives.

Spanish Olive Commission

Famous French Cookery

BOEUF À LA MODE

- 2 tablespoons butter or margarine
- 4 pound beef rump roast, rolled and tied
- ¼ cup chopped onion
- 2 cups dry white wine
- ½ cup hot water
- 1½ teaspoons salt
- ½ teaspoon thyme
- ¼ teaspoon freshly ground pepper
- 3 whole cloves
- ½ bay l
  Spr
- 12 small white onions, peeled
- 6 medium carrots, pared and quartered lengthwise
- 2 tablespoons flour

1. Melt butter over medium-high heat in a Dutch oven. Add beef and brown well on all sides. This should take about 30 minutes. During last few minutes of browning, add chopped onion.
2. Add wine, water, salt, thyme, pepper, cloves, bay leaf and parsley. Bring to a boil. Reduce heat and simmer, covered, 2½ hours.
3. Add whole onions and carrots. Cover and simmer 1 hour or just until beef is fork tender.
4. Remove beef to a heated serving platter. Lift out vegetables with a slotted spoon and place around beef. Keep warm.
5. Skim off excess fat from top of cooking liquid. Combine ¼ cup cold water with the flour. Gradually stir into liquid in Dutch oven. Bring to a boil and cook, stirring constantly, until mixture is smooth and thickened. Strain gravy and serve with meat and vegetables.
6. Makes 8 to 10 servings.

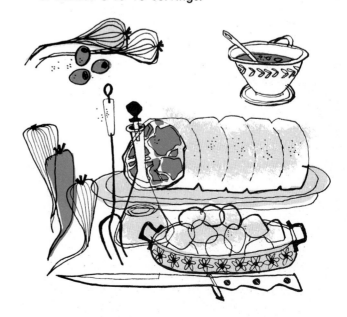

BEEF BOURGUIGNONNE MARINER

3 pounds beef chuck or top round, cut into
  2-inch cubes
1 small onion, sliced
2 cups red wine
1 small bay leaf
4 sprigs parsley
  Pinch of thyme
2 tablespoons salad oil
½ teaspoon salt
¼ teaspoon freshly ground black pepper
1 small carrot, sliced
1 clove garlic, crushed
3 tablespoons butter or margarine, divided
1 tablespoon flour
½ cup beef consommé
¼ pound salt pork, diced
24 small white onions, peeled
½ pound whole fresh mushrooms

1. In a deep bowl combine beef, sliced onion, wine, bay leaf, parsley, thyme, oil, salt, pepper, carrot and garlic. Let stand at least 4 hours, turning occasionally. Remove beef and pat dry with paper towels. Strain marinade and reserve for later use.
2. Heat 2 tablespoons butter in a Dutch oven. Add beef and brown well on all sides. Remove beef and stir in flour. Cook, stirring constantly, for about 2 minutes. Stir in consommé and marinade. Return beef to pan and bring to a boil. Cover and simmer about 2 hours.
3. While beef is cooking, heat remaining 1 tablespoon butter in a small skillet. Add salt pork and white onions. Cook over medium heat about 10 minutes, or until pork and onions are golden brown. Scrape salt pork bits, onions and fat in pan into Dutch oven with meat. Add mushrooms. Cover and simmer 45 minutes or until meat is fork tender.
4. Serve with plain boiled potatoes.
5. Makes 6 to 8 servings.

CARBONNADES FLAMANDE

2 pounds dry onions
  Butter
3 pounds chuck or round steak, cut in cubes
  Flour
  Salt and pepper
3 cloves garlic
1 cup beer

1. Peel and slice onions. Melt about 4 tablespoons butter in a Dutch oven. Cook onion until soft and lightly browned. Remove onion.
2. Dust chuck cubes with a little flour. Melt 4 tablespoons butter in Dutch oven. Add cubes and brown over high heat. Return onion to Dutch oven.
3. Season with salt and pepper. Add garlic and beer.
4. Cover tightly and simmer about 1¼ hours or until beef is tender.
5. Mix together 2 tablespoons flour with 2 tablespoons cold water to make a paste. Drop into sauce in small pieces. Cook, stirring, until sauce thickens slightly and comes to a boil. Taste and add more salt and pepper if desired.
6. Makes 6 servings.

DAUBE PROVENÇALE

5 pound rump of beef
3 or 4 slices salt pork
2 pig's feet or 1 calf's foot
2 bay leaves
8 cloves garlic
1 whole clove
1 strip orange peel
1 teaspoon rosemary
  Several sprigs parsley
1 tablespoon salt
2 teaspoons freshly ground black pepper
  Red wine
  Cooked macaroni

1. Place beef in a large bowl or casserole. Add salt pork, pig's feet, bay leaves, garlic, clove, orange peel, rosemary, parsley, salt and pepper. Cover meat with red wine. Cover bowl with aluminum foil and let stand for at least 24 hours.
2. Place meat and marinating ingredients in a heavy casserole or Dutch oven.
3. Heat oven to 200°F.
4. Cook about 6 hours or until meat is tender.
5. Remove meat to a hot serving platter. Let stand for about 15 minutes before slicing.
6. Skim excess fat off liquid in pan. Strain sauce and serve part of it with cooked macaroni, a traditional accompaniment for this dish.
7. This is excellent served cold. Strain the sauce and let it cool. Slice the meat and arrange on a serving platter. Cover with sauce. Place in refrigerator and allow the sauce to jell over slices of meat.
8. Makes 8 to 10 servings.

BEEF TENDERLOIN

1 whole beef tenderloin, 4 to 6 pounds
  Salad oil
  Garlic

1. Heat oven to 450°F.
2. Remove surface fat and connective tissue from beef tenderloin. Place on a rack in a shallow roasting pan. Turn narrow end of tenderloin under to make the roast an even thickness.
3. Rub top of meat with cut clove of garlic. Brush with oil or cover top with strips of suet.
4. Insert a meat thermometer into the center of the thickest part of the meat.
5. Roast 45 to 60 minutes or until meat thermometer registers rare.
6. Cut in slices about 1-inch thick and serve with wine or mushroom sauce.
7. Makes 8 to 10 servings.

FILET DE BOEUF, DUC DE ROQUEFORT

½ cup celery, coarsley chopped
1 small onion, sliced
1 bay leaf, crumbled
¼ teaspoon dried rosemary
3½ to 4 pound filet of beef
    Butter
    Salt
    Pepper
2 tablespoons cognac
3 cups sifted flour
½ cup shortening
    Ice water
½ pound Roquefort cheese
1 egg yolk
1 tablespoon milk
1 cup veal stock or chicken bouillon
1 truffle, minced (optional)

1. Heat oven to 450°F.
2. Place celery, onion, bay leaf and rosemary in the bottom of a baking pan.
3. Cover filet with a generous coating of butter. Sprinkle with salt and freshly ground black pepper. Place on top of celery mixture in baking pan. Bake 30 minutes.
4. Remove filet from oven. Warm cognac and pour over top of filet. Ignite with a match and allow flames to burn out. Let meat stand in pan and cool completely while preparing pastry covering.
5. Sift together flour and 1 teaspoon salt into a mixing bowl. Cut in shortening with a pastry blender or two knives to the consistency of cornmeal. Add about 4 tablespoons ice water, or enough to make the dough stick together. Shape into a ball, wrap in waxed paper and chill.
6. On a lightly floured board, roll dough into a rectangle about ⅛-inch thick.

7. Remove filet from pan, leaving vegetables in pan. Force Roquefort cheese through a sieve and mix it into a paste. Spread cheese over top and sides of filet.
8. Place filet on center of pastry. Wrap pastry around filet, trimming edges as needed. Secure ends with a bit of cold water.
9. Place filet on a baking sheet. Beat together egg yolk and milk. Brush top of pastry with egg yolk mixture.
10. Bake 15 minutes or until pastry is nicely browned.
11. While filet is baking, remove as much fat as possible from top of vegetables in roasting pan. Add veal stock and place over medium heat. Simmer, stirring constantly to bring up all browned bits of meat from bottom of pan. Strain mixture into a saucepan.
12. Chop truffle and add to sauce. Let simmer about 15 minutes to blend flavors. Stir in 1 tablespoon softened butter just before serving.
13. Remove filet to a heated serving platter. Cut in generous slices and serve with truffle sauce.
14. Makes about 6 to 8 servings.

BEEF SCALLOP FLAMBÉ

1½ pound filet of beef
4 tablespoons butter
2 tablespoons salad oil
¼ cup cognac
    Salt and pepper
¼ cup chopped shallots
½ cup finely snipped parsley
2 tablespoons Worcestershire sauce
2 tablespoons chili sauce
3 tablespoons Madeira

1. Cut filet of beef in thin slices similar to veal slices used in veal scallopini.
2. Heat butter and oil in a heavy skillet over very high heat. Add scallops and fry very quickly, to brown on both sides. This should take about 2 minutes. Warm the cognac. Pour over meat and ignite with a match. Let flames burn out. Season to taste with salt and pepper. Remove to a hot serving platter. Keep warm.
3. Pour most of the fat out of skillet. Add shallots, parsley, Worcestershire sauce, chili sauce and Madeira. Bring to a boil and simmer 2 minutes. Season to taste. Pour over beef on platter.
4. Makes 4 to 6 servings.

In France the beef carcass is cut in a different manner than here at home. French butchers follow muscle separations for cutting the carcass while American butchers cut cross grain, leaving the bones on in many cases. Because the cuts are different, it may help to explain some of the names you will see on French menus or in some of the recipes.

Entrecote: A steak cut from the rib roast section, similar to our rib or club steak.

Rumsteck: Cut from the end of the rump.

Contre Filet: A steak cut from the loin of beef. This particular piece of meat is usually left on in American markets and sold as part of a Porterhouse or T-Bone steak.

In France the whole filet of beef is removed from the animal and cut into three different parts. In America you will occasionally find filets on sale; however, usually you will have to put in a special order to the butcher.
   1. The large end, or the sirloin end, is considered the least tender in France and is called Bifteck.
   2. The middle section is cut into steaks about 2 inches thick and called Chauteaubriand. A 1-inch steak cut from this section becomes a filet.
   3. The skinny end of the filet or that found in the T-bone section is cut into Tournedos and wrapped in salt pork strips or slices of bacon. The even smaller end is cut into Filet Mignon, and is considered the most tender.

BEEF WELLINGTON

1 recipe pastry
1 whole beef tenderloin, 4 to 6 pounds
1 clove garlic, halved
   Salt and pepper
4 pieces suet or 6 strips bacon
   Forcemeat Filling or Chicken Liver Pâté
3 to 4 truffles, optional
1 egg, lightly beaten
   Sauce Madeira

1. Prepare pastry (recipe follows).
2. Heat oven to 450°F.
3. Rub the filet all over with the cut side of garlic. Sprinkle with salt and pepper. Cover with suet or bacon strips, securing with string if necessary. Place on rack in roasting pan. Insert meat thermometer into thickest part of filet.
4. Roast 45 to 50 minutes or until meat thermometer registers rare.
5. Cool meat slightly. Remove suet and place meat in refrigerator until final preparation.
6. Heat oven to 425°F.
7. On a lightly floured board roll pastry into an 18-by 18-inch square or large enough to enclose beef.
8. Lay beef along one edge of pastry. Cover with forcemeat or pâté. Cut truffles in halves and place along the top in a line. Lift pastry up over beef, overlapping it under meat and sealing edges. Trim off a few small ends of pastry for garnish. Brush edges with beaten egg to seal.

9. Carefully place beef on baking sheet, sealed edge down.
10. Cut decorative shapes from pastry trimmings and arrange down center of pastry. Brush all over with beaten egg.
11. Bake about 30 minutes or until pastry is cooked and lightly browned.
12. Remove carefully with two broad spatulas to a hot serving platter. Cut in fairly thick crosswise slices and serve plain or with Sauce Madeira.
13. Makes 10 to 12 servings.

PASTRY

4 cups flour
1 teaspoon salt
½ cup butter
½ cup shortening
1 egg, lightly beaten
   Ice water

1. Place the flour, salt, butter and shortening in a mixing bowl. Blend together with a pastry blender or fingertips until mixture resembles large bread crumbs. Add egg and enough ice water to make mixture form a ball. Wrap in waxed paper and chill in refrigerator.
2. This should be made in advance and can be made the day before final preparation.

Beef Wellington is a classic French dish for a very, very special occasion. Tenderloin of beef is covered with forcemeat or pâté and baked in a crust.

Brussel Sprouts Marketing Program

FORCEMEAT

¼ cup butter or margarine
¼ cup chopped onion
½ cup chopped mushrooms
¼ cup cognac
½ pound finely ground veal
½ pound finely ground pork
1 egg, lightly beaten
¼ cup heavy cream
¼ cup chopped parsley
1 teaspoon salt
¼ teaspoon basil
¼ teaspoon thyme
¼ teaspoon rosemary
⅛ teaspoon ground allspice
⅛ teaspoon pepper

1. Melt butter in a small saucepan. Add onion and cook until onion is tender but not browned. Stir in mushrooms and cognac and cook over medium heat 5 to 10 minutes.
2. Turn mixture into a large bowl. Add remaining ingredients and mix lightly but thoroughly.
3. Cover and refrigerate until ready to use.

SAUCE MADEIRA

2 tablespoons butter or margarine
2 tablespoons finely chopped shallots
1½ cups canned beef gravy
2 tablespoons lemon juice
¼ cup Madeira

1. Melt the butter in a small saucepan over medium heat. Add shallots and cook until tender but not browned.
2. Add gravy and lemon juice and bring to a boil. Stir in Madeira and heat thoroughly.
3. Makes 1½ cups sauce.

CHICKEN LIVER PÂTÉ

6 tablespoons butter
¼ cup chopped shallots
2 cloves garlic, finely chopped
1 pound chicken livers
¼ cup cognac or Madeira
4 thin slices ham, diced
Salt and pepper

1. Melt butter in a heavy skillet over medium heat. Add shallots and garlic and cook until tender but not browned.
2. Turn heat to high. Add chicken livers and cook quickly until browned on all sides. Add cognac and stir to scrape up browned particles from bottom of skillet.

3. Add diced ham and simmer 2 minutes. Cool.
4. Turn mixture out onto a chopping board and chop very fine or put mixture through a meat grinder. Add salt and pepper to taste.

FONDUE BOURGUIGNONNE

1 cup butter
1 cup salad oil
Sauces
2½ pound filet of beef, well trimmed and cut into ½-inch cubes

1. Place butter and oil in fondue pan. Place over medium heat and heat to 375°F.
2. Place fondue pan on stand over canned heat flame. Keep oil sizzling hot during cooking time.
3. On the table place bowls of as many different dipping sauces as desired.
4. Serve each person a plate containing raw chunks of beef. Give each person 2 forks, one two-pronged fondue fork and one dinner fork. Pierce a chunk of meat with the fondue fork. Hold meat in the hot oil and brown according to taste; rare, medium or well done will take from 10 to 30 seconds.
5. Transfer meat to dinner fork, dip cooked meat into a sauce of choice and eat. Meanwhile, spear another cube of meat with fondue fork and place in hot oil.
6. Makes 6 to 8 servings.

BÉARNAISE SAUCE

¼ cup tarragon vinegar
¼ cup dry white wine or dry Vermouth
2 teaspoons tarragon leaves
1 tablespoon chopped shallots
½ cup butter or margarine
1 egg
¼ teaspoon salt
Pinch of cayenne

1. Combine vinegar, wine, tarragon leaves and shallots in a small stainless steel or earthenware saucepan. Cook over low heat until mixture is reduced to 2 tablespoons. Remove from heat, cool slightly.
2. Melt butter in the top of a double boiler over hot, not boiling water. Be sure that the bottom of the double boiler does not touch the water.
3. Add egg, salt, cayenne and reduced liquid. Beat with a wire whisk until mixture is smooth and thick.
4. Remove from hot water at once.
5. Makes ¾ cup sauce.

BLENDER BÉARNAISE SAUCE

2 tablespoons dry white wine
1 tablespoon tarragon vinegar
2 teaspoons dried tarragon
2 teaspoons minced shallots
½ cup butter
3 egg yolks
¼ teaspoon pepper
2 tablespoons lemon juice
¼ teaspoon salt

1. In a small saucepan combine the wine, vinegar, tarragon and shallots. Bring to boil and cook rapidly until almost all the liquid disappears.
2. In a small saucepan heat the butter until it is bubbling, but do not brown.
3. In the container of an electric blender place the egg yolks, pepper, lemon juice and salt. Cover the container and flick the motor on and off at high speed.
4. Remove cover, turn motor on high and gradually add the bubbling butter. Add the herb mixture, cover and blend very quickly on high speed.
5. Makes about 1 cup sauce.

MUSTARD SAUCE

¼ cup prepared mustard
¼ cup mayonnaise
1 clove garlic, crushed
¼ teaspoon Tabasco

1. Combine all ingredients. Refrigerate until ready to serve.
2. Makes about ½ cup sauce.

TOMATO-MUSHROOM SAUCE

⅔ cup catsup
2 tablespoons chopped cooked or canned mushrooms
¼ teaspoon Tabasco

1. Combine all ingredients. Refrigerate until ready to serve.
2. Makes about ½ cup sauce.

SAUCE SMETANE

¾ cup dairy sour cream
1 to 2 tablespoons grated horseradish
Salt and pepper

1. Combine the sour cream with the prepared horseradish. Season to taste with salt and pepper. There is a wide difference among various prepared horseradish sauces — some are mild whereas others are very strong — so taste often while preparing

sauce. Refrigerate until ready to serve.
2. Makes about ¾ cup sauce.

TOURNEDOS

6 tournedos wrapped with bacon
 Olive oil
 Finely chopped garlic
 Finely chopped parsley
1 cup dry white wine
 Salt and pepper
6 slices fried bread (preferably French bread)

1. Place tournedos in an ovenproof glass pie dish. Top with enough oil to moisten each steak. Sprinkle with garlic and parsley. Let stand in the refrigerator 24 hours.
2. Heat a heavy skillet over very high heat. Sear tournedos quickly in hot skillet on both sides. Dribble in wine, a little at a time, so that the tournedos will go on cooking and not drown in the wine. When tournedos are done to your liking, remove and place each one on a slice of fried bread.
3. Serve with sauce from skillet.
4. Makes 6 servings.

STEAK DIANE

4 sirloin strip steaks, cut ½-inch thick
 Salt
 Freshly ground black pepper
1 teaspoon dry mustard
¼ cup butter
3 tablespoons lemon juice
2 teaspoons snipped chives
1 teaspoon Worcestershire sauce

1. With a meat mallet or the bottom of a heavy saucepan, pound steaks to ⅓ inch thickness. Sprinkle one side of each steak with salt, pepper and ⅛ teaspoon dry mustard. Pound mixture into meat. Repeat with other side of meat.
2. Melt butter in skillet over medium high heat.
3. When butter is very hot add steaks and cook 2 minutes on each side. Remove steak to a hot serving platter.
4. Add lemon juice, chives and Worcestershire sauce to drippings in skillet. Bring to boil. Pour over meat.
5. Makes 4 servings.

Note: For a very special party touch, Steak Diane may be prepared at the dinner table in a chafing dish or electric skillet.

QUICK WINE STEAKS

1 package (1 ounce) beef gravy mix
1 cup beef bouillon
1 cup dry red wine
1 tablespoon red currant jelly
6 thin, tender steaks, cut just less than ½ inch thick
1 teaspoon salt
¼ teaspoon pepper
¼ cup butter or margarine

1. Prepare beef gravy mix according to directions on the package, using 1 cup beef bouillon. Stir in wine and jelly. Heat and stir until jelly dissolves.
2. Sprinkle steaks with salt and pepper.
3. Heat butter in a large, heavy skillet over high heat. Brown steaks very quickly in hot butter. Pour wine sauce over steaks and cook over high heat 3 to 4 minutes, or until steaks are cooked to desired degree of doneness.
4. Makes 6 servings.

FRENCH STEAKS

2 tablespoons butter
1½ tablespoons salad oil
2 pounds beef steak, ¾ to 1 inch thick
½ cup beef bouillon or dry red wine
2 tablespoons softened butter

1. Put butter and oil in a heavy skillet over high heat. When the butter has foamed and begins to subside it is right for the steak.
2. Cut steak in 4 pieces, or use 4 cuts of small steak. Fry steak on one side 3 to 4 minutes. Turn steak and brown on other side 3 to 4 minutes, depending on desired degree of doneness. Test for doneness by cutting a small incision in the steak.
3. Remove steak to a hot platter and season with salt and pepper. Keep warm.
4. Pour fat out of skillet. Add bouillon or dry red wine and cook over high heat. Scrape up brown bits from bottom of the pan and boil until liquid is reduced almost to a syrup. Remove from heat and stir in butter until it has melted. Pour sauce over steak.
5. Makes 4 servings.

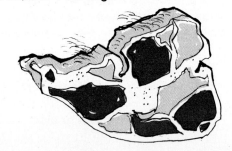

PEPPER STEAK

3 pound boneless sirloin steak
3 tablespoons whole peppercorns
1 tablespoon salad oil
2 tablespoons butter, divided
½ cup dry red wine
2 tablespoons brandy
1 teaspoon salt

1. Wipe steak with a damp paper towel. Place peppercorns on a board and crush with a rolling pin, or crush in a mortar and pestle. Pat crushed peppercorns on both sides of steak, so that they stick to steak.
2. Heat a large, heavy skillet over high heat. Add oil and 1 tablespoon butter. When foam begins to subside, add steak. Brown on both sides, about 2 minutes on each side. Reduce heat to medium and cook about 8 minutes on each side for medium rare. Make a small slit in steak to check for doneness, and cook to your own taste.
3. Remove steak to a hot serving platter and keep warm.
4. Add remaining butter, wine, brandy and salt to skillet. Simmer, stirring, about 3 minutes. Pour sauce over steak.
5. Makes 6 servings.

BEEF ROULADES WITH ROQUEFORT

(shown opposite)

6 cubed beef steaks, about 1½ pounds
1 teaspoon salt
¼ teaspoon pepper
½ cup crumbled Roquefort cheese, packed
1 can (3 ounces) mushroom pieces
1 tablespoon minced onion
2 tablespoons flour
2 tablespoons shortening
1 can (12 ounces) vegetable juice cocktail
1 tablespoon Worcestershire sauce

1. Sprinkle steaks with half of the salt, pepper and Roquefort cheese.
2. Drain mushrooms, reserving juice. Combine mushrooms, onion and remaining salt and pepper. Sprinkle mixture over Roquefort cheese on steaks.
3. Roll up steaks and fasten securely with wooden picks. Dredge rolls in flour.
4. Heat shortening in a large skillet over medium heat. Brown rolls well on all sides in hot fat. Pour off as much fat as possible from the skillet.
5. Combine juice drained from mushrooms,

vegetable juice cocktail and Worcestershire sauce. Pour mixture around beef. Cover skillet tightly and cook over low heat 40 minutes or until tender.

6. Remove roulades to a heated platter. Stir remaining Roquefort cheese into sauce in pan. Cook, stirring to bring up browned bits from bottom of pan, until sauce is blended. Pour sauce over roulades.

7. Makes 6 servings.

BEEF ROULADES

2½ pounds round steak
¾ pound ground pork
1 teaspoon poultry seasoning
¾ teaspoon salt
½ clove garlic, crushed
2 tablespoons finely chopped onion
¼ cup soft white bread crumbs
8 slices bacon
3 tablespoons butter or margarine
8 small white onions, peeled
⅓ cup flour
1 can (10 ounces) beef bouillon
2½ cups dry red wine
1½ pounds fresh mushrooms
1 bay leaf

1. Cut round steak into 8 equal-sized pieces, ⅛ inch thick.
2. Combine ground pork, poultry seasoning, salt, garlic, onion and bread crumbs. Toss lightly.
3. Place about 2 tablespoons of mixture on each piece of beef. Roll up. Wrap each roll with a slice of bacon and tie with heavy thread.
4. Melt butter in a Dutch oven over medium high heat. Brown beef rolls on all sides in hot butter. Remove meat from Dutch oven. Add onion and brown lightly all over. Remove onion. Remove Dutch oven from heat.
5. Stir in flour. Gradually stir in bouillon and wine. Return to medium heat and cook, stirring constantly, until mixture comes to a boil. Return meat and onion to Dutch oven. Add mushrooms and bay leaf. Simmer over low heat 1½ to 2 hours, or until meat is tender. If sauce gets too thick during cooking time, thin with a little more red wine.
6. Before serving, remove thread from beef roulades. Serve with onions and mushrooms and gravy from pan.
7. Makes 4 to 6 servings.

To someone visiting France for the first time, it comes as a surprise to find that French people adore hamburgers. Their hamburgers are made from lean beef and mixed with a variety of other ingredients. They are usually pan-fried, much as steak, and finished off with a sauce.

However, a popular innovation from America is hamburger quick lunch counters and restaurants. The French enjoy a quick hamburger on a bun, with a cup of coffee or a soft drink, much as we do here. But most Frenchmen do not pick up a hamburger and bun in the hands, as we do, but leave it on the plate and eat it with fork and knife. The favorite in Paris is a hamburger with a fried egg on top, which may account for the use of knife and fork!

FRENCH HAMBURGER

¼ **cup finely minced onion**
Butter
1½ **pounds ground lean beef**
1½ **teaspoons salt**
⅛ **teaspoon pepper**
⅛ **teaspoon thyme**
1 **egg, lightly beaten**
Flour
1 **tablespoon salad oil**
½ **cup beef bouillon or dry red wine or white wine**

1. Cook onion in about 2 tablespoons butter until tender but not browned. Scrape onion and butter into a mixing bowl.
2. Add beef, salt, pepper, thyme and egg. Mix lightly to blend thoroughly. Form into patties about ¾ inch thick.
3. Just before cooking, dust patties lightly with flour.
4. Place 1 tablespoon butter and salad oil in skillet over high heat. When foam begins to subside, add patties and fry 2 to 3 minutes on each side, or longer if well done meat is preferred.
5. Remove patties and place on a warm serving platter. Keep warm.
6. Pour off all fat from skillet. Add liquid and boil rapidly, scraping brown bits from bottom of pan. When liquid is reduced almost to a syrup remove from heat. Stir in about 2 tablespoons softened butter. Pour sauce over hamburgers.
7. Makes 4 to 6 servings.

WINE BURGERS

1 **pound ground chuck**
½ **cup dry red wine, divided**
1 **teaspoon salt**
⅛ **teaspoon pepper**
2 **tablespoons snipped parsley**
2 **tablespoons snipped chives**

1. Combine chuck, ¼ cup red wine, salt and pepper. Mix lightly. Shape into 4 patties.

2. Heat butter in a skillet over medium high heat. Fry patties on both sides to the desired degree of doneness. Remove patties and place on heated serving dish.
3. Pour off fat from skillet. Add remaining wine, parsley and chives. Cook over high heat about 1 minute, stirring up browned bits from bottom of pan. Pour sauce over patties.
4. Makes 4 servings.

GROUND STEAK PARISIAN

2½ **pounds ground lean beef**
Salt and pepper
⅔ **cup crumbled Roquefort cheese**
¼ **cup butter**
½ **pound mushrooms, sliced**
1¼ **cups dry red wine**

1. Season beef lightly with salt and pepper. Mix lightly. Divide into 12 oval patties. Divide Roquefort cheese evenly on 6 of the patties. Place remaining patties on top of cheese and seal edges.
2. Melt 2 tablespoons butter in a skillet. Add mushrooms and brown lightly. Remove mushrooms.
3. Add remaining butter to skillet. Brown meat patties on both sides in hot butter.
4. Return mushrooms to skillet. Add wine and simmer, uncovered, 5 minutes, basting meat constantly. Serve immediately.
5. Makes 6 servings.

SUZETTE'S MEATBALLS

1 cup fresh bread crumbs
2 tablespoons milk
Butter
2 onions, chopped
1½ pounds chuck, ground twice
2 egg yolks
1 teaspoon curry powder
¼ teaspoon sage or thyme
¼ teaspoon mace
¼ teaspoon marjoram or oregano
¼ teaspoon tarragon or basil
Salt and pepper
Dry bread crumbs
2½ cups dairy sour cream
1 teaspoon lemon juice
Chopped dill or parsley

1. Combine fresh bread crumbs and milk and set aside.
2. Melt 4 tablespoons butter in a small skillet. Add onion and sauté until golden brown.
3. In a mixing bowl combine ground chuck, egg yolks and cooked onion. Squeeze any excess milk from bread crumbs and add crumbs to meat. Add seasonings. Mix thoroughly with your hands. Shape mixture into small even balls. Press a small lump of firm butter into center of each ball. Roll balls in dry bread crumbs. Pat well in hands so the crumbs will stick. Chill for 30 minutes so that crumbs will stick to the meatballs a little better.
4. Melt 4 tablespoons of butter in a large skillet. Add meat balls and cook until golden brown on all sides and cooked through. Remove meatballs to a hot serving dish and keep warm.
5. Pour off almost all the fat from the skillet. Stir in the sour cream, lemon juice and chopped dill. Heat, scraping bits from bottom of skillet, but do not boil. Taste for seasoning. Pour sauce over meatballs.
6. Makes about 6 servings.

STEAK TARTARE

1 pound sirloin or round steak
½ cup finely chopped green onion
4 egg yolks
Minced onions
Capers
Chopped parsley
Salt
Freshly ground black pepper
Pumpernickel or rye bread

1. Have butcher remove all fat from meat and have meat put through the grinder twice.
2. Place meat in a bowl, add green onion and toss lightly with a fork.
3. Divide meat and pile lightly on 4 serving plates. Make an indentation in the center and slip in a raw egg yolk. Garnish with minced onion, capers and parsley.
4. Serve with salt, freshly ground black pepper and thinly sliced pumpernickel or rye bread.
5. Makes 4 servings.

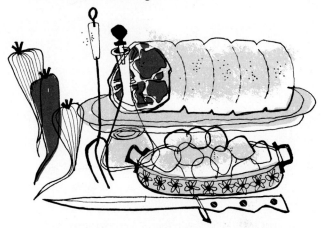

MUSHROOM WINE BURGERS

1 pound ground chuck
¼ cup cream
¼ cup milk
1 tablespoon minced onion
1 teaspoon salt
¼ teaspoon pepper
2 tablespoons butter or margarine
2 tablespoons flour
½ cup beef bouillon
½ cup red dinner wine
1 teaspoon Worcestershire sauce
2 tablespoons chopped parsley
1 can (4 ounces) sliced mushrooms
3 or 4 slices toast

1. Combine chuck, cream, milk, onion, salt and pepper. Toss lightly with a fork. Shape into 3 or 4 thick patties.
2. Pan fry patties in hot butter in a skillet just until browned on both sides. Remove patties and keep warm.
3. Add flour to the drippings in the skillet. Stir in bouillon and wine. Cook, stirring constantly, until mixture boils and thickens. Add Worcestershire sauce, parsley and mushrooms with liquid. Season to taste with salt and pepper.
4. Return patties to sauce and simmer until meat is cooked to the desired degree of doneness.
5. Place meat patties on toast and pour sauce over the top.
6. Makes 3 or 4 servings.

Desserts

When it comes to desserts, the French have a reputation for some of the best in the world. Nothing is more tempting than a tray of luscious French pastry made up of cream puffs, Napoleons and cream-filled or fruit-topped tarts. The French are famous for dessert soufflés, high and puffy, served piping hot and often laced with flavorful liquors. Flaming desserts rate high for restaurant fare, but Cherries Jubilee and flaming Crepes Suzettes can also be made at home.

However, do not dream blissfully of having gorgeous desserts like this every night of the week. You will find that most French people eat fruit and cheese for dessert at home and if they have anything sweet it is likely to be a simple pudding. Fancy French pastries are usually bought at the bakery which even in small towns has a wondrous display of the baker's art. Flaming desserts are reserved for dining out or for very special occasions.

ROUE AUX MARRONS
(shown opposite)

6 eggs
1½ cups sugar, divided
1 cup sifted flour
Butter
½ teaspoon almond extract
1 teaspoon grated lemon rind
1 cup confectioners' sugar
2 tablespoons kirsch
1 can (15¾ ounces) unsweetened chestnut purée
Water
2 squares (2 ounces) unsweetened chocolate
2 tablespoons rum
2 teaspoons grated orange rind.

1. Break eggs into a mixing bowl and let stand until they reach room temperature.
2. Heat oven to 350°F.
3. Grease the bottoms of 2 9-inch layer cake pans. Cut 2 9-inch circles of waxed paper. Place in bottom of pans and grease waxed paper.
4. With an electric mixer beat eggs until foamy. Gradually beat in 1 cup sugar, 2 tablespoonsful at a time. Beat until mixture resembles whipped cream and holds soft peaks. Sift flour over top of eggs and fold in carefully with a rubber scraper. Fold in ¼ cup melted butter, almond extract and lemon rind.
5. Divide batter between 2 prepared pans. Bake 25 to 30 minutes or until top springs back when lightly touched in the center with the fingers. Loosen edges of cake layers with a sharp knife and turn out on a cake rack to cool. Remove waxed paper before cooling. Cool thoroughly before frosting.
6. Cream ½ cup butter until light and fluffy. Gradually stir in confectioners' sugar, kirsch and chestnut purée. Beat until smooth and shiny. Spread half the filling over the top of one layer. Top with second layer. Put remaining frosting in pastry bag. Garnish top and sides of cake with frosting,

as shown.
7. Combine water and ½ cup sugar in a saucepan and boil for 5 minutes. Add chocolate and stir until chocolate is melted. Cool sauce. Stir in rum and orange rind.
8. To serve, cut cake in serving pieces. Pass sauce to pour over top of cake.
9. Makes one 9-inch cake.

VACHERIN

6 egg whites
2 cups sugar
¼ teaspoon salt
1½ teaspoons lemon juice
2 pints vanilla ice cream, softened
1 cup heavy cream
½ cup diced marrons glace (preserved chestnuts)

1. Heat oven to 275°F.
2. Draw 2 circles, each 9 inches in diameter, on heavy brown paper. Place the paper on a baking sheet.
3. Beat egg whites until stiff. Gradually beat in combined sugar and salt. Add lemon juice alternately with last ½ cup of the sugar. Continue beating until mixture is very stiff and glossy.
4. Divide egg white mixture between the circles on brown paper, spreading it out to the edges of the circles, and smoothing the surface.
5. Bake 1 hour and 15 minutes. Remove from oven and let cool on brown paper.
6. Slip a long thin spatula between the meringue and paper to loosen without breaking. Place one layer on a flat cake plate or tray. Spread with 1 pint softened ice cream. Whip cream until stiff and spread half of cream over ice cream. Sprinkle with half the marrons. Repeat, using second layer, ice cream, whipped cream and maroons.
7. Set Vacherin in freezer until ready to serve. Do not hold for more than 1 hour. Use a thin, sharp knife to cut into wedge-shaped pieces.

BÛCHE DE NOËL

4 eggs, separated
1⅔ cups sugar, divided
½ teaspoon vanilla
1 cup sifted cake flour
½ teaspoon baking powder
¼ teaspoon salt
3 tablespoons rum, divided
⅓ cup water
2 egg yolks
½ cup butter or margarine, softened
1½ squares unsweetened chocolate, melted
1 teaspoon instant coffee powder

1. Heat oven to 375°F.
2. Grease the bottom of a 15½- by 10½- by 1-inch jelly roll pan. Dust the greased surface with flour. Shake off excess flour.
3. Beat the egg yolks until thick and lemon colored. Gradually add ½ cup sugar, beating constantly. Stir in vanilla.
4. In large mixer bowl, beat the egg whites until soft peaks form. Gradually add ½ cup sugar, beating until egg whites stand in stiff peaks.
5. Gently fold egg yolk mixture into egg white mixture. Sift together flour, baking powder and salt. Sift over top of egg mixture and fold in gently.
6. Spread mixture evenly in prepared jelly roll pan. Bake 10 to 12 minutes or until top springs back when lightly touched.
7. Loosen edges of cake. Immediately turn out onto a kitchen towel that has been liberally sprinkled with confectioners' sugar. Sprinkle cake evenly with 2 tablespoons rum. Roll up cake and towel, starting at long side. Cool.
8. In a small saucepan combine ⅔ cup sugar and water. Bring to a boil and cook to 240°F. on a candy thermometer or to the soft ball stage.
9. In a small mixing bowl, beat egg yolks until thick and lemon colored. Very gradually add the hot syrup, beating constantly. Continue beating until mixture is completely cool. Beat in the softened butter, 1 tablespoonful at a time. Add chocolate and remaining rum and instant coffee powder. Continue beating until thick.
10. Unroll cake. Spread evenly with half of the filling. Roll cake up starting at long side. Cut a 4-inch piece from end of roll, cutting on the diagonal. On a serving platter, place 4-inch piece along side of large roll, at an angle to look like a tree branch. Frost with remaining filling. Mark frosting with tines of fork to resemble bark on a tree.

GÉNOISE HÉLÈNE

4 eggs
½ cup sugar
1½ teaspoons vanilla, divided
Dash of salt
1 cup sifted cake flour
½ cup butter, melted and cooled
1 can (1 pound 13 ounces) pear halves
½ cup apricot preserves
1 package (6 ounces) semi-sweet chocolate pieces
2 cups dairy sour cream, divided
¼ cup confectioners' sugar
¼ teaspoon grated nutmeg

1. Heat oven to 350°F.
2. Generously butter the bottom of two 8-inch round cake pans. Dust with flour. Set aside.
3. Place eggs, sugar, 1 teaspoon vanilla and salt in a mixing bowl which can be set in a larger bowl filled with hot water. Beat until very light and fluffy and doubled in volume (about 5 minutes with an electric mixer).
4. Remove bowl from water and continue beating until stiff peaks form and mixture is glossy (about 10 minutes on high speed with an electric mixer).
5. Sift one third of the flour over batter and very gently fold into the mixture. Repeat with second third of the flour and then last third of flour. Very carefully fold in melted butter.
6. Divide batter in half between the two prepared cake pans. Bake 35 to 40 minutes or until top springs back when touched lightly with fingers.
7. Remove from oven and cool on wire racks for 5 minutes. Turn out of pans onto racks to cool completely.
8. Drain pears, reserving syrup. In a small bowl mix together ¼ cup of the syrup with the apricot preserves. Set aside for glaze.
9. Melt chocolate pieces over hot water. Cool slightly. Stir in 1 cup of the sour cream until well blended. Set aside for glaze.
10. To assemble genoise, split each cake layer in half, crosswise. Place bottom half of a layer on a cake plate. Spread with a thin coating of the apricot glaze. Spread with 3 tablespoons of the chocolate-sour cream mixture. Add top half of layer and repeat coating of glaze and chocolate. Repeat with second layer, spreading some glaze and chocolate mixture on top and sides of cake. Place in refrigerator to chill.
11. In a chilled bowl, with chilled beaters, beat remaining cup of sour cream until doubled

in volume. This will take about 5 minutes. Fold in confectioners' sugar, ½ teaspoon vanilla and nutmeg.

12. Remove cake from refrigerator. Arrange 6 pear halves, cut side down, on top of génoise with narrow ends towards center. Fill in center and between pears with sour cream mixture. Chill about ½ hour before serving.

13. Dice remaining pears. Fold into remaining sour cream mixture and serve as a sauce with the génoise.

14. Makes 12 servings.

COUQUES

½ cup warm water (105-115°F)
1 package or cake yeast, active dry or compressed
2¼ cups unsifted flour, divided
½ cup butter or margarine, melted
3 eggs, beaten
¼ cup sugar
½ teaspoon salt
2 cans (1 pound each) pear halves, drained
¼ cup dark brown sugar, firmly packed
¼ cup butter or margarine
½ teaspoon cinnamon
½ teaspoon nutmeg
Whipped cream

1. Measure warm water into a large warm bowl. Sprinkle or crumble in yeast; stir until dissolved. Stir in ½ cup flour. Cover and let rise in a warm place, free from draft, about 30 minutes.

2. Blend in 1½ cups flour, ½ cup melted butter, eggs, sugar and salt. Beat until well blended. Cover and let rise in a warm place, free from draft, until doubled in bulk, about 1 hour.

3. Stir batter down. Cover and refrigerate at least 2 hours.

4. Grease twelve 10-ounce deep pie dishes. Place about ¼ cup batter in each dish. Using well floured hands, pat mixture around dishes, bringing it about 1 inch up the side of each dish. Place a pear half, cut side up, in each dish.

5. Combine remaining ¼ cup flour, and brown sugar in a small bowl. Cut in butter with a pastry blender or two knives. Stir in cinnamon and nutmeg. Sprinkle mixture over top of pears.

6. Let rise, uncovered, free from draft, about 30 minutes.

7. Heat oven to 375°F.

8. Bake about 15 minutes, or until done.

9. Remove from dishes and serve warm topped with whipped cream.

10. Makes 12 couques.

ROQUEFORT CHEESE CAKE

1 tablespoon butter or margarine, softened
⅓ cup packaged cereal crumbs
2 tablespoons flour
½ cup sugar, divided
5 packages (3 ounces each) cream cheese, softened to room temperature
½ cup crumbled Roquefort cheese, packed
3 eggs, separated
½ cup dairy sour cream
Dash of salt
2 teaspoons grated lemon rind
Strawberry Glaze

1. With softened butter, thoroughly butter sides and bottom of a 9-inch spring form pan. Sprinkle buttered surface with cereal crumbs.

2. Heat oven to 325°F.

3. In a bowl combine flour and half the sugar. Add cream cheese and Roquefort cheese and beat until smooth and fluffy.

4. Beat egg yolks until light. Blend the eggs into the cheese mixture. Stir in sour cream, salt and lemon rind.

5. Beat egg whites until soft peaks form. Gradually beat in remaining sugar; continue beating until stiff. Fold egg whites into cheese mixture. Pour into pan.

6. Bake 45 to 60 minutes or until cake is firm in the center. Turn off heat. Let stand in oven for 45 minutes.

7. Cool at room temperature and then chill.

8. Cover top with Strawberry Glaze. Loosen sides of pan and place on serving dish.

9. Makes 8 servings.

STRAWBERRY GLAZE

1 pint strawberries, washed and sliced
⅓ cup strawberry jelly
1 tablespoon cornstarch
¼ teaspoon cinnamon
⅓ cup water

1. Crush ½ cup of the sliced berries. In a saucepan combine crushed berries, jelly, cornstarch, cinnamon and water. Cook over low heat, stirring constantly, until mixture is smooth and clear. Strain sauce and cool slightly.

2. Arrange remaining berries over top of cheesecake. Spoon cooled mixture over top of berries, coating them evenly.

3. Chill at least 1 hour before serving.

GÂTEAU MARIGNAN

Water
2 packagaes or cakes yeast, active dry or compressed
2 cups unsifted flour
4 eggs, slighly beaten
Sugar
½ teaspoon salt
⅔ cup margarine, softened
1 jar (10 ounces) strawberry jelly
1½ cups heavy cream
2 cups sliced fresh strawberries

1. Measure ½ cup warm (105-115°F) water into a small warm bowl. Sprinkle or crumble in yeast. Stir until dissolved.
2. Place flour in a large bowl. Add eggs and dissolved yeast. Beat for 2 minutes.
3. Cover bowl and let rise in a warm place free from draft, about ½ hour or until bubbly and doubled in bulk.
4. Stir down. Add 1 tablespoon sugar, salt and softened margarine. Beat until well mixed and dough is elastic when dropped from a spoon, about 4 minutes. Turn into a well greased 3-quart ring mold. Let rise in a warm place, free from draft, about ½ hour or until doubled in bulk.
5. Heat oven to 450°F.
6. Bake 10 to 12 minutes or until done. Cool a few minutes, then turn out of ring mold and cool.
7. Form a basket by cutting inner ring from top of cake. Cut this thin ring in half for handles.
8. Melt jelly with 1 tablespoon water in a small saucepan. Brush over cake and handles.
9. Place handles on cake across the center at an angle so that they support each other like handles on a basket. Use toothpicks for added support if necessary.
10. Whip cream until stiff. Add 2 tablespoons sugar and beat just until well blended. Fold in strawberries.
11. Place cake on a serving platter. Fill center with cream mixture. Serve immediately.

GÂTEAU AUX CERISES

2 packages (3 ounces each) cream cheese, softened
¼ cup butter or margarine
½ cup sugar
2 teaspoons grated orange peel
1 teaspoon salt
3 eggs
Water
1 package or cake yeast, active dry or compressed
2¼ cups unsifted flour
½ cup orange marmalade
1 can (1 pound) cherry pie filling
Vanilla ice cream

1. Cream together cream cheese and butter until light and fluffy. Add sugar, grated orange peel, salt and eggs. Beat until very well blended.
2. Measure ¼ cup warm (105-115°F) water into a small warm bowl. Sprinkle or crumble in yeast. Stir until dissolved.
3. Add yeast and flour to cream cheese mixture. Beat until very well blended.
4. Cover top of bowl. Let rise in a warm place, free from draft, about 1 hour or until doubled in bulk.
5. Beat batter down and spoon into a greased 6½-cup ring mold. Let rise in a warm place, free from draft, about 1 hour or until doubled in bulk.
6. Heat oven to 375°F.
7. Bake ring 20 to 25 minutes or until done. Cool. When cold turn out onto a serving plate.
8. Combine orange marmalade and 1 tablespoon water. Cook over medium heat until marmalade becomes thin and begins to boil. Brush on cake.
9. Combine cherry pie filling and ½ cup water. Stir until blended.
10. Fill center of the cake with vanilla ice cream. Top with cherry sauce.

BABA AU RHUM

¼ cup milk
¼ cup warm water (105-115°F.)
1 package or cake yeast, active dry or
   compressed
¼ cup butter or margarine, softened
¼ cup sugar
3 eggs
2 cups unsifted flour
Rum Sauce

1. Put milk in a small saucepan and heat just until bubbles appear around edge of pan. Cool to lukewarm.
2. Measure warm water into large warm mixer bowl. Sprinkle or crumble in yeast. Stir until dissolved. Add milk, butter, sugar, eggs and flour. Blend at low speed of electric mixer for one minute, then beat 2 minutes at medium speed. Scrape down sides of bowl. Cover bowl and let rise in a warm place, free from draft, for 30 minutes.
3. Beat batter down with a wooden spoon. Spoon mixture into a greased 9-inch ring mold. Cover and let rise in a warm place, free from draft, until doubled in bulk.
4. Heat oven to 350°F.
5. Bake ring mold 30 minutes or until done.
6. Immediately prick surface with a fork, before removing from pan. Slowly pour rum sauce over cake. After syrup in absorbed, turn cake out on a serving plate.

RUM SAUCE

½ cup sugar
⅓ cup water
¼ cup rum

1. Combine sugar and water in a small saucepan. Bring to a boil.
2. Remove from heat and stir in rum. Pour over Baba.

Puff Paste

The pride and joy of every pastry chef and home baker is puff paste. It is the basis for many mouthwatering delicacies on the French pastry tray in a good restaurant. It can be fashioned into circles and filled with cream or jams. Pieces folded in half are filled with fruit or jams. Tiny shells can be filled with custard or berries. Of course the favorite of all, strips of delicate puffed pastry sandwiched together with custard, are Napoleons, or "little cakes of a thousand layers".

Puff paste is not easy to make, but is certainly well worth the effort if you have the time and the will. The secret of puff paste is the layering of butter between layers of pastry which as it is turned and folded incorporates air between the layers. When the pastry is placed in a hot oven, the trapped air expands and makes the pastry flaky and delicate. The making of puff paste is time consuming, because it must rest and chill between rollings and turnings. But the main secret is to prevent the butter from breaking through the pastry as you are turning and rolling. Your first attempt may be utter disaster, but if you persevere you will become an expert and be able to produce the finest of all French pastry.

PUFF PASTE (PÂTÉ FEUILLETÉ)

4 cups unsifted flour
½ teaspoon salt
1 pound sweet butter, chilled
1 cup ice water

1. Mix together flour and salt in a large bowl. Cut ½ pound of the butter into small pieces and add to flour mixture. Chill remaining butter. With a pastry blender, cut butter into flour until mixture is like coarse cornmeal.
2. Add ice water to flour mixture, stirring lightly with a fork. Stir just until mixture is blended. Shape into a ball. Wrap in foil or waxed paper and chill for 30 minutes.
3. Put dough on a lightly floured board and using a floured rolling pin roll dough into a rectangle about ½ inch thick.
4. Dot center third of dough with bits of remaining chilled butter. Fold over both ends of dough to cover butter in center. Press edges together to seal in as much air as possible. Wrap in waxed paper and chill in refrigerator about 20 minutes.
5. Place dough on a lightly floured board and roll into a rectangle about ½ inch thick. Roll lightly to be sure that none of the butter pops through the dough while rolling. Turn the rectangle so that it is horizontal, then fold dough into thirds, crosswise again. Roll dough out to ¼-inch thickness and fold in thirds again. Wrap lightly in waxed paper and chill in refrigerator 10 to 20 minutes.
6. Roll dough, turn and fold twice more as in Step 5, being sure to chill between rolling.
7. Dough may now be used immediately or chilled in the refrigerator over night. Dough will keep well in refrigerator for several days.
8. Puff paste can be made into many shapes and has many uses. Probably the best known are Pastry Shells and Napoleons.

PASTRY SHELLS

1. Roll out puff paste on a lightly floured board to ¼-inch thickness. Cut in 2-inch circles with a floured cutter, plain or fluted. Cut the center from half the circles to make rings. Brush the edges of the whole circles with water and place a ring on top of each. Press each circle and ring gently together and put them on a baking sheet covered with a double thickness of brown paper. Brush the rings with beaten egg and replace the tiny circle cutouts lightly in each ring. Chill in the refrigerator for 30 minutes.
2. Heat oven to 425°F. Bake 20 to 25 minutes or until puffed and golden brown.
3. When cool, remove the tops and fill shells with fresh berries, custard or jam. (Cut in larger circles, they can be used as a main course, filled with creamed chicken or crab meat.)

NAPOLEONS

1 recipe Puff Paste
1 package (3⅝ ounces) vanilla pudding and pie filling mix
1½ cups milk
½ cup heavy cream
Confectioners' sugar

1. Heat oven to 425°F.
2. Divide puff paste in half. Return half of pastry to refrigerator and use for other sweets. Carefully divide the pastry in thirds. On a floured board, lightly roll one third of the dough into a 12-inch square. Place carefully on a baking sheet that is covered with two thicknesses of brown paper.
3. Prick top of pastry generously with a fork and chill about 10 minutes.
4. Bake 20 to 25 minutes or until pastry is dry and golden brown.
5. Carefully remove to a flat surface and bake remaining thirds of dough in the same manner. You will now have three rectangles of baked pastry.
6. Cook pudding according to directions on package, using 1½ cups milk. Cover top of pudding with a piece of waxed paper and chill in the refrigerator.
7. When pudding is chilled, whip cream until stiff. Fold cream into chilled pudding and blend until mixture is smooth.
8. Place 1 pastry rectangle on baking sheet. Cover with half of pudding mixture. Cover with second pastry rectangle and spread with remaining pudding. Top with third pastry rectangle and sprinkle with confectioners' sugar.
9. Refrigerate for 1 hour. With a very sharp knife, cut it in thirds crosswise. Cut each third into 6 slices.
10. Makes 18 small napoleons.

MINARETS

½ cup butter or margarine
1 cup boiling water
½ teaspoon salt
1 cup sifted flour
4 eggs
1 package (6 ounces) semi-sweet chocolate morsels
6 tablespoons evaporated milk
1 package (8 ounces) cream cheese
¼ cup sugar
2 teaspoons vanilla

1. Heat oven to 400°F.
2. In a medium sized, heavy saucepan, heat butter with boiling water over high heat, stirring occasionally, until butter is melted.
3. Turn heat to low. Add salt and flour all at once. Stir vigorously over low heat, until mixture leaves side of pan in a smooth compact ball. Remove from heat.
4. Add eggs, one at a time, beating with a wooden spoon until smooth after each addition. Continue beating until mixture has a satin-like sheen.
5. For base of each minaret, spoon 8 mounds of the mixture on a greased baking sheet, using about 2 tablespoons of the mixture for each. For top of each minaret, spoon 8 mounds of the mixture onto baking sheet, using about 1 teaspoon mixture for each.
6. Bake small puffs about 20 to 25 minutes. Bake large puffs about 40 to 45 minutes or until puffed and lightly browned.
7. Remove from baking sheets and cool.
8. Melt semi-sweet chocolate morsels over hot, not boiling water. Remove from heat and cool slightly.
9. Gradually add evaporated milk to cream cheese and blend until smooth. Stir in sugar and vanilla. Stir in melted chocolate. Chill until mixture is of spooning consistency.
10. Cut puffs in half. Spoon filling into bottom half of large puffs. Place large puff tops on filling hollow side up. Spoon in more filling. Fill small puffs and place on top.
11. Place in freezer and freeze until ready to serve. Sprinkle with confectioners' sugar before serving.
12. Makes 8 servings.

FRENCH CHEESECAKE PUFF

¼ cup butter or margarine
½ cup hot water
¼ teaspoon salt
2 tablespoons sugar
  Pinch of cinnamon
½ cup sifted flour
2 eggs
1 cup creamed cottage cheese
½ cup sugar
¼ cup heavy cream
  Grated rind of 1 lemon
  Juice of 1 lemon

1. Heat oven to 400°F.
2. Place butter, hot water, salt, sugar and cinnamon in a medium saucepan. Bring to a boil over high heat.
3. Turn heat to low. Dump in flour all at once and stir vigorously until mixture leaves sides of pan and becomes a smooth, compact ball.
4. Remove from heat and beat in eggs, one at a time, until smooth. Continue beating with a spoon until mixture is smooth and shiny.
5. Grease a baking sheet. Spread mixture out on baking sheet into a circle about 10 inches in diameter. Mound mixture around edge of circle to make an edge that will puff up during baking.
6. Press cottage cheese through a sieve to make a smooth mixture. Stir in sugar, cream, lemon rind and juice. Pour mixture into center of circle.
7. Bake about 35 minutes or until mixture is puffed up and lightly browned.
8. Serve warm.
9. Makes 6 to 8 servings.

CHOCOLATE ECLAIRS

1 cup water
½ cup butter or margarine
¼ teaspoon salt
1 cup sifted flour
4 large eggs
  Chocolate Nut Filling

1. Heat oven to 400°F.
2. In a large saucepan bring water, butter and salt to a boil. Add flour all at once and cook over medium heat, stirring constantly, until mixture leaves sides of pan and forms a ball of dough.
3. Remove from heat and stir in eggs one at a time, beating well after each addition. Continue beating until mixture is smooth and glossy.
4. Separate dough into egg-size balls. Place on greased baking sheet. Using spoons, stroke and stretch each ball into an eclair-shaped rod about 4 inches long.
5. Bake 30 to 35 minutes or until eclairs are puffed up and lightly browned. Remove from oven and turn off heat. Make a slit in the side of each puff to allow steam to escape. Return to oven and let stand about 10 minutes with oven door ajar.
6. Remove from baking sheet and cool on wire rack.
7. When cool, cut eclair shells in half lengthwise. Remove any moist dough in center. Fill with Chocolate Nut Filling. Dust tops with confectioners' sugar if desired.
8. Makes about 12 large eclairs.

CHOCOLATE NUT FILLING

1 package (3⅝ ounces) chocolate nut pudding
1 cup heavy cream
1 cup milk

1. Prepare pudding according to package directions, using heavy cream and milk.
2. Cool. Use to fill eclairs.

ELEGANT CREAM PUFFS

½ cup water
¼ cup butter or margarine
¼ teaspoon salt
½ cup sifted flour
2 large eggs or 3 small eggs
  Sour Cream Filling
  Chocolate Glaze

1. Heat oven to 400°F.
2. In a large saucepan bring water, butter and salt to a boil. Add flour all at once and cook over medium heat, stirring constantly, until mixture leaves sides of pan and forms a ball of dough.
3. Remove from heat and stir in eggs, one at a time, beating well after each addition. Continue beating until mixture is smooth and glossy.
4. Mound batter on a greased baking sheet into 6 mounds at least 2 inches apart.
5. Bake 30 to 35 minutes or until puffs are high and lightly browned. Remove from oven and turn off heat. Make a slit in the side of each puff to allow steam to escape. Return to oven and let stand about 10 minutes with oven door ajar.
6. Remove from baking sheet and cool on wire rack.
7. To serve, split puffs in half. Scoop out any moist dough in center. Fill with Sour Cream Filling and top with Chocolate Glaze.
8. Makes 6 large puffs.

SOUR CREAM FILLING

½ cup sugar
⅓ cup sifted flour
1½ cups milk
2 eggs, slightly beaten
1 tablespoon butter
½ teaspoon vanilla
1 cup dairy sour cream

1. In a large heavy saucepan combine sugar and flour. Slowly stir in milk. Cook over medium heat, stirring constantly, until mixture comes to a boil. Remove from heat.
2. Stir a small amount of the hot milk into beaten eggs. Return egg mixture to milk in saucepan and stir well. Cook over low heat, stirring constantly, until mixture comes to a boil. Remove from heat immediately.
3. Stir in butter and vanilla. Turn mixture into a bowl. Cover the surface of the custard by pressing a piece of waxed paper directly on the surface of the pudding. Chill in the refrigerator.
4. When mixture is cooled, beat with a rotary beater until fluffy. Fold in sour cream. Use to fill cream puffs.

CHOCOLATE GLAZE

¼ cup cocoa
½ cup confectioners' sugar
¼ cup milk

1. In a small bowl, combine cocoa and confectioners' sugar. Blend in milk. Stir until mixture is smooth. Drizzle over top of filled cream puffs.
2. Chill puffs until ready to serve.

PETIT FOURS

2¼ cups sifted cake flour
1 cup sugar
2 teaspoons baking powder
1 teaspoon salt
½ cup margarine, softened
1 teaspoon vanilla
2 eggs
¾ cup milk, divided
1 jar apricot or pineapple preserves
Confectioners' Sugar Icing

1. Heat oven to 350°F.
2. Grease the bottom of a 15½- by 10½- by 2-inch jelly roll pan. Cover with a sheet of waxed paper. Grease top of paper.
3. Sift together flour, sugar, baking powder and salt into the large bowl of an electric mixer. Add margarine, vanilla, eggs and ½ cup milk. Beat 2 minutes at medium speed, scraping sides and bottom of bowl constantly with a rubber scraper.
4. Add remaining milk and beat 2 minutes longer. Scrape bowl occasionally.
5. Pour into prepared pan, spreading dough out evenly.
6. Bake about 25 minutes or until cake springs back when touched lightly with the fingers.
7. Remove from oven and cool slightly. Turn out onto a cake rack and remove waxed paper. Cool.
8. Cut cake into fancy shapes. Use cookie cutter for 2½-inch rounds or cut out 2-inch squares. Cut rectangles about 2½- by 1½-inches. Arrange pieces in pairs, flat sides together.
9. Spread bottom piece with preserves, then press top into place gently. Frost with confectioners' sugar icing. Top with finely chopped nuts, chocolate or colored sprinkles.
10. Makes 16 petit fours.

CONFECTIONERS' SUGAR ICING

½ cup margarine, softened
Salt
½ teaspoon vanilla
2 cups confectioners' sugar
2 to 3 tablespoons hot milk

1. In the small bowl of an electric mixer combine margarine, pinch of salt, vanilla and confectioners' sugar. Add about 1 tablespoon hot milk. Beat at high speed about 10 minutes, gradually adding more milk until of smooth spreading consistency.
2. Makes about 1 cup icing.

ELEGANT PARTY ECLAIRS

½ cup water
¼ cup margarine or butter
⅛ teaspoon salt
½ cup sifted flour
2 eggs
Chocolate Filling
Confectioners' sugar

1. Heat oven to 400°F.
2. In a saucepan combine water, margarine and salt. Bring to a boil. Remove from heat and add flour all at once. Cook over low heat, stirring constantly, until mixture leaves the sides of the pan and forms a ball.
3. Remove from heat. Add eggs, one at a time, beating until smooth and glossy after each addition.
4. Fit a pastry bag with a number 7 plain tube. Fill pastry bag with mixture. Press out eclairs, about 2 inches long, onto a greased baking sheet. Leave about 2 inches of space between each eclair.
5. Bake 15 to 20 minutes or until golden brown and crisp.
6. Remove from oven and cool slightly. Cut a slice from top of each eclair and carefully remove dough or filament inside. Cool.
7. To serve, fill with with Chocolate Filling and dust tops with confectioners' sugar.
8. Makes about 27 tiny eclairs.

CHOCOLATE FILLING

⅔ cup sweetened condensed milk
1 square unsweetened chocolate
⅛ teaspoon salt
¼ cup water
¼ teaspoon vanilla
½ cup heavy cream, whipped

1. Combine milk, chocolate and salt in top of a double boiler. Cook over rapidly boiling water until chocolate melts. Continue cooking, stirring constantly, until mixture is very thick, about 5 minutes. Gradually stir in water, keeping mixture smooth. Continue cooking, stirring constantly, until mixture thickens again.
2. Remove from heat and stir in vanilla. Refrigerate until ready to fill eclairs.
3. Before filling eclairs, fold whipped cream into chocolate mixture.
4. Makes about 1⅓ cups filling.

French pastries and more! A handsome array of Petit Fours, Elegant Party Eclairs, Easy "French" Pastries, Chocolate Mousse and Mincemeat crêpes.

The Borden Co.

CHOCOLATE MOUSSE

2 teaspoons unflavored gelatine
 Cold water
1 can (15 ounces) sweetened condensed milk
3 squares unsweetened chocolate
3 eggs, separated
1 teaspoon vanilla
2 tablespoons cognac

1. Soften gelatine in ¼ cup cold water.
2. In top part of double boiler combine sweetened condensed milk and chocolate. Cook over boiling water until chocolate melts. Continue cooking, stirring, until mixture is smooth and very thick, about 5 minutes. Gradually stir in ½ cup water, keeping mixture smooth.
3. Beat egg yolks slightly. Stir a small amount of the hot mixture into egg yolks. Return egg mixture to top of double boiler. Cook over hot water, stirring constantly, until mixture is smooth and thick, about 5 minutes.
4. Remove from heat and stir in softened gelatine, vanilla and cognac. Stir until gelatine is dissolved. Cool to room temperature.
5. Beat egg whites until they stand in stiff peaks. When chocolate mixture mounds slightly when dropped from a spoon, fold in egg whites.
6. Pour mixture into a 5-cup mold which has been very lightly oiled.
7. Refrigerate about 3 hours or until firm.
8. Unmold on a serving dish and serve with whipped cream, if desired.
9. Makes about 6 servings.

EASY "FRENCH" PASTRIES

1 package (9½ ounces) flaky refrigerator biscuits
1 can (15 ounces) sweetened condensed milk
⅓ cup lemon juice
½ teaspoon vanilla
½ teaspoon almond extract
 Canned fruit such as apricot halves or canned cherry pie filling, or fresh fruit such as strawberries or blueberries.
1 jar currant jelly, optional

1. Heat oven to 375°F.
2. Open packaged biscuits according to package directions. Carefully split each biscuit in half crosswise.
3. Press each biscuit half into a tiny tart pan, about 2½-inch diameter, to make pastry shell. Press a small piece of aluminum foil over top of shell and fill with dried beans or peas. Place shells on a baking sheet.

4. Bake 8 minutes. Remove from oven. Remove foil and beans from each shell. Return shells to oven and bake about 5 minutes longer or until inside of shells are slightly brown and firm.
5. Remove from oven and cool slightly. Take shells from pans and cool thoroughly before filling.
6. In a mixing bowl combine sweetened condensed milk, lemon juice, vanilla and almond extract. Stir until well blended and thickened. Spoon mixture into cooled shells. Refrigerate 30 minutes or longer.
7. Top each pastry with either canned or fresh fruit. If desired, melt currant jelly over low heat and dribble a little on top of each pastry for a pretty glaze. Refrigerate until ready to serve.
8. Makes 20 tarts.

MINCEMEAT CRÊPES

5 tablespoons sifted flour
½ teaspoon sugar
¼ teaspoon salt
2 eggs
1 cup milk
 Salad oil
 Confectioners' sugar
1 package (9 ounces) condensed mincemeat
¾ cup water
1 cup orange juice
3 tablespoons Grand Marnier, divided

1. In a medium-sized mixing bowl blend flour, sugar and salt. In another bowl beat eggs slightly and then beat in milk. Pour egg mixture into flour mixture and beat with a wire whisk until thoroughly blended. Let stand at least 1 hour.
2. Heat a small skillet, about 5½-inch diameter bottom, over medium high heat. Brush with a light coat of salad oil. Pour in about 1 tablespoon batter, tilting pan to cover entire bottom. Cook until lightly browned. Loosen edge slightly with thin spatula, pick up edges with fingers and flip crêpe over on other side. Remove crêpes and stack in a pile, sprinkling each one with a little confectioners' sugar to keep from sticking.
3. Crumble mincemeat into a small saucepan. Add water and stir over medium heat until lumps are broken. Bring to a brisk boil and boil 1 minute.
4. Pour mixture into a chafing dish or skillet. Add orange juice and 2 tablespoons Grand Marnier. Heat. Turn each crêpe into the sauce and fold in quarters, using a fork and

a spoon. When all the crêpes are folded and turned, warm the remaining Grand Marnier. Pour carefully over crêpes and ignite with a match. Spoon sauce over crêpes while it is flaming.

5. Serve immediatley on heated dessert dishes.
6. Makes 6 servings of 2 crêpes each.

DESSERT CRÊPES

1 cup plus 2 tablespoons sifted flour
4 tablespoons sugar
Pinch of salt
3 eggs, beaten
1½ cups milk
1 tablespoon melted butter
1½ tablespoons cognac

1. Combine flour, sugar and salt in a bowl. Beat together the eggs and milk. Stir into flour mixture and beat until smooth. This can be done on low speed of a mixer or with a wire whisk. Stir in melted butter and cognac. Let mixture stand for at least 2 hours before cooking.
2. Heat a small skillet, about 5½-inches diameter across the bottom, over medium high heat.
3. When skillet is hot add ½ teaspoon butter and swirl around pan to cover sides and bottom.
4. Pour in 1 full tablespoon batter. Rotate and tilt pan very quickly to spread batter over bottom of skillet. This must be done before batter has a chance to set.
5. Cook crêpe about 1 minute, or until it is set and browned on one side. Loosen sides with spatula and flip crêpe over quickly with the fingers. Lightly brown second side. The second will not brown as nicely as the first side, so it is usually turned inside when it is rolled or folded.
6. Roll crêpes, fold them into quarters, or stack them on top of each other. They may be served immediately with a sprinkle of confectioners' sugar, fresh fruit or a sauce. They may also be used in other dishes such as Crêpes Suzette.
7. Makes 20 to 24 crêpes.

CRÊPES SUZETTE

6 lumps sugar
1 orange
½ cup butter
1 tablespoon lemon juice
¼ cup Curacao or Cointreau
¼ cup Grand Marnier
1 receipe dessert crêpes
½ cup warm brandy

1. Rub sugar lumps on the skin of the orange until they are covered with the aromatic oil. Crush the lumps and blend well with the butter. Squeeze the juice from the orange and reserve.
2. In a chafing dish or flat skillet melt the butter and sugar mixture. Add orange juice, lemon juice, Curacao and Grand Marnier. Bring mixture to a boil.
3. One by one place the crêpes in the sauce, spoon the sauce over them so they are moistened on both sides, and fold in quarters.
4. Pour warm brandy carefully over crêpes. Ignite with a match.
5. Serve crêpes on heated plates while sauce is still blazing.
6. Makes 6 to 8 servings.

CRÊPES DIRECTOIRES

6 bananas
½ cup finely chopped almonds
12 dessert crêpes
6 tablespoons butter
4 tablespoons sugar
¼ cup Grand Marnier
⅓ cup warm cognac

1. Heat oven to 350°F.
2. Bake bananas in their skins 18 to 20 minutes.
3. Split banana peel and remove bananas. Split in half, lengthwise.
4. Sprinkle chopped almonds over top of crêpes. Roll a crêpe around each banana half.
5. Melt butter and sugar in a chafing dish or large flat skillet. When mixuture starts to caramelize, add crêpes. Then add Grand Marnier and heat crêpes in sauce.
6. Carefully pour on cognac. Ignite with a match and spoon syrup over top of crêpes.
7. Serve on warm dessert plates with sauce over top.
8. Makes 6 servings.

CRÊPES AUX FRAISES

1 package (9 ounces) cream cheese
1 cup dairy sour cream
3 boxes (10 ounces each) frozen
   strawberries, defrosted
3 tablespoons butter
3 tablespoons grated orange rind
2 tablespoons lemon juice
3 tablespoons Cointreau
3 tablespoons brandy
18 to 20 dessert crêpes

1. Heat oven to 350°F.
2. Cream together cheese and sour cream until light and smooth. Set aside.
3. Press strawberries through a sieve to remove the seeds. Put pulp in a saucepan, add the butter, orange rind and lemon juice. Bring to a boil and boil 1 minute. Set aside.
4. Spread each crêpe with part of the cream cheese mixture. Roll up and place side by side in a shallow casserole. Do not stack crêpes.
5. Add Cointreau and brandy to strawberry sauce. Spoon a small amount of the sauce over crêpes in the casserole.
6. Bake 15 minutes. Serve with remaining heated strawberry sauce.
7. Makes 6 to 8 servings.

FRENCH LEMON WAFERS

½ cup butter or margarine
½ cup sugar
2 teaspoons grated lemon peel
1 tablespoon lemon juice
⅛ teaspoon salt
3 unbeaten egg whites
1 cup sifted flour

1. Heat oven to 400°F.
2. Cream together butter, sugar, lemon peel, juice and salt until light and fluffy.
3. Add egg whites alternately with the flour, beating well after each addition.
4. Force mixture through a pastry tube or drop by teaspoonsful about 1 inch apart on greased baking sheets.
5. Bake about 10 minutes until or edges are lightly browned.
6. Remove from baking sheets and cool on wire racks.
7. Makes about 3½ dozen wafers.

CRÊPES JUBILEE
(shown opposite)

1 can (1 pound 5 ounces) cherry pie filling, divided
4 tablespoons kirschwasser
1 recipe desert crêpes

1. Combine 1 cup cherry pie filling with 2 tablespoons of the kirschwasser. Spread 1 heaping teaspoon of the pie filling mixture on one side of a crêpe and roll up. Repeat with remaining crêpes.
2. Place rolled crêpes in a 9½- to 10-inch flat crêpe pan or a large heat-proof platter. Pour remaining pie filling around rolled crêpes. Place crêpe pan or platter on an alcohol burner stand.
3. Heat remaining 2 tablespoons kirschwasser. Pour carefully over crêpes and ignite with a match. Allow flames to burn out.
4. Serve crêpes with sauce immediately.
5. Makes about 10 servings.

ALMOND WAFERS

¾ cup butter or margarine, softened
1½ cups sugar, divided
1 teaspoon grated lemon rind
2 egg yolks
1½ cups sifted flour
⅛ teaspoon almond flavoring
1 cup blanched, sliced almonds
¼ teaspoon nutmeg
1 egg white
1 tablespoon water

1. Heat oven to 375°F.
2. Cream butter with 1 cup sugar and lemon rind until light and fluffy. Beat in egg yolks, one at a time. Stir in almond flavoring. Add flour and stir until well blended. Chill dough until firm.
3. Combine almonds with remaining sugar and nutmeg. Beat egg white with water until foamy.
4. With the fingers, shape dough into ½-inch balls. Place on greased baking sheets. Flatten balls with the bottom of a glass that has been dipped in sugar. Brush top of cookies with egg white. Sprinkle almond mixture on top of cookies.
5. Bake 8 to 10 minutes or until edges are lightly browned.
6. Remove to wire racks to cool.
7. Makes about 5 dozen wafers.

MADELEINES

¾ cup sweet butter
2 eggs
¾ cup sugar
½ teaspoon grated lemon rind
½ teaspoon vanilla extract
1 cup unsifted flour

1. Put butter in a small, deep saucepan. Heat slowly until foam on top of butter disappears and there is a light brown sediment on the bottom of the pan. Remove from heat and skim off any brown bits on top of butter. Carefully pour off clear butter, leaving sediment in pan. Set butter aside.
2. Heat oven to 450°F.
3. Put eggs, sugar and lemon rind in a flat mixing bowl, and stir just until blended. Place bowl over a saucepan containing hot water. Water should not touch the bottom of the bowl nor should it boil. Place saucepan over low heat until egg mixture is lukewarm.
4. Remove bowl from hot water and beat with an electric mixer at high speed until light, fluffy and tripled in volume. Add vanilla.
5. Fold in flour and butter carefully. Do not beat.
6. Butter ¾-inch madeleine pans. Fill two-thirds full with batter.
7. Bake 7 to 8 minutes or until golden brown. Let stand about 2 minutes. Turn out of pans. Butter pans again, refill with batter and bake. Repeat until all batter is used.
8. Serve madeleines upside down to show the fluted pattern.
9. Makes about 40 madeleines.

Flans

The dessert flan is a tart or open-faced pie, consisting of a straight-sided pastry shell and a sweet fruit filling, plain or with a custard base. The fruit is arranged attractively and covered with a clear glaze.

Pastry for a flan is usually richer and "shorter" than the crust for an American pie. It is high in butter or shortening content, often contains sugar, and occasionally an egg. It is sometimes hard to work with, but it is easy to patch up, and when it is filled, no one will ever see the patches.

A flan ring is merely a ring of metal, usually aluminum, that is placed on a baking sheet. After baking, the ring is removed and the shell stands alone since the crust is usually much thicker than our pie crust. If you do not have a flan ring, here are directions for making one: Tear off a strip of heavy-duty aluminum foil 17 inches long. Divide in half to make two 17-inch strips. Fold each to form a 1¼-inch strip, then join ends to form a 9-inch circle. Remove foil ring before serving.

FLAN PASTRY

1 cup sifted flour
1 egg yolk
1 tablespoon sugar
½ cup slightly softened butter
Grated rind of 1 lemon
Pinch of salt
Ice water

1. Sift flour into a mixing bowl. Make a well in center of flour and add egg yolk, sugar, butter cut into small pieces, lemon rind and salt. Mix ingredients in center into a paste with fingers. Quickly work in the flour, adding a very little ice water, if needed, to moisten the dough so that it can be gathered together into a ball.
2. Wrap dough in waxed paper and chill in refrigerator for at least an hour.
3. When dough is well chilled, place on a lightly floured board. Flour rolling pin and roll dough lightly from the center out to the edge. Lift dough and turn occasionally, flouring bottom if necessary to keep it from sticking. Roll dough into a circle about 2" larger than pan.
4. Place dough very carefully in pan. Either roll it gently over a rolling pin and place over top of pan, or fold dough in half, then in half again. Unroll or unfold over pan.
5. Press dough gently into bottom of pan and fit carefully around edges without pulling it. Press dough against sides to make it stick. Make a small decorative edge around top of pan with dough. If dough breaks, take small pieces of dough and press down over breaks.
6. Some recipes call for filling to be placed in unbaked shell. Refrigerate shell while making filling.
7. To make a baked shell, line the dough with a piece of aluminum foil. Fill with dried beans or rice. Bake in hot oven (400°F.) 10 minutes. Reduce heat to moderate (350°F.) and bake 10 minutes. Remove shell from oven, take out foil and beans. Prick bottom of shell with fork. Return shell to oven and bake 5 to 10 minutes or until shell is baked and lightly browned. Remove ring. Cool before filling.
8. Makes 1 9-inch shell.

STRAWBERRY FLAN

⅓ cup sugar
¼ cup cornstarch
¼ teaspoon salt
1¾ cups milk
2 eggs, beaten
¼ teaspoon grated lemon rind
¼ teaspoon vanilla
1 9-inch baked flan shell
2 pints fresh strawberries
⅓ cup red currant jelly

1. Mix together sugar, cornstarch and salt in a heavy saucepan. Slowly blend in milk. Cook over medium heat, stirring constantly, until mixture thickens and boils for 30 seconds.
2. Stir a small amount of the hot mixture into beaten eggs. Return egg mixture to saucepan. Cook over low heat, stirring constantly, until very thick and smooth.
3. Remove from heat and stir in lemon rind and vanilla. Cool. Press a piece of waxed paper directly on surface of custard to prevent skin forming. Chill in refrigerator.
4. Spread chilled custard filling in tart shell. Clean and hull berries. Place berries as close together on surface of custard as possible.
5. Put jelly in a small saucepan and heat until melted. Spoon over strawberries. Chill.
6. Makes 8 servings.

A Strawberry Flan is so pretty that it is a shame to cut it. But do—you will find the pastry covered with a rich custard and topped off with strawberries.

California Strawberry Advisory Board

PEACH FLAN

Whipped topping mix (enough to make 2 cups)
½ cup cold milk
½ cup sugar
2 cups cottage cheese
1½ teaspoons vanilla
½ cup chopped almonds
1 can (1 pound 13 ounces) sliced peaches
1 9 inch baked flan shell
1 tablespoon cornstarch
2 teaspoons lemon juice
⅛ teaspoon mace

1. Combine whipped topping and milk. Beat until topping stands in a stiff peaks. Gradually add sugar and blend well.
2. Put cottage cheese in blender and blend until smooth. If you do not have a blender, put cottage cheese through a fine sieve.
3. Fold cottage cheese, vanilla and almonds into whipped topping.
4. Drain peaches and save syrup. Cut slices in half lengthwise.
5. Put half of the whipped topping mixture into baked flan shell. Arrange half the peaches over filling. Spoon remaining topping mixture over peaches. Arrange remaining peaches on the top in an attractive pattern. Chill thoroughly.
6. Measure 1 cup peach syrup into a saucepan. Add cornstarch, lemon juice and mace and blend well.
7. Cook over medium heat, stirring constantly, until syrup thickens. Cool. Spoon glaze over peaches on top of flan. Chill 2 to 3 more hours before serving.
8. Makes 1 9-inch flan.

PEACH-PLUM FLAN

Sugar
⅓ cup flour
¼ teaspoon salt
2 cups milk
2 egg yolks, beaten
2 tablespoons butter
1 teaspoon vanilla
1 9-inch baked flan shell
1 tablespoon water
1 cup diced red plums
½ teaspoon lemon juice
2 fresh peaches, peeled and sliced or
1 package (12 ounces) frozen sliced peaches, thawed and drained

1. In a heavy saucepan mix together ⅔ cup sugar, flour and salt. Gradually stir in milk.

Cook over medium heat, stirring constantly, until mixture boils. Boil 1 minute and remove from heat. Stir a small amount of hot mixture into egg yolks. Return egg yolk mixture to hot cooked mixture and blend well. Cook over low heat, stirring constantly, just to the boiling point.
2. Remove from heat and stir in butter and vanilla. Cool slightly. Pour into baked flan or pie shell. Chill in the refrigerator.
3. In a small saucepan combine ¼ cup sugar and 1 tablespoon water. Bring to a boil. Add plums and simmer until mixture thickens, stirring often.
4. Remove from heat and stir in lemon juice. Put mixture through a sieve and cool.
5. Arrange peach slices on top of cooled filling in flan shell. Pour plum mixture over top of peaches. Chill before serving.
6. Makes 6 to 8 servings.

UPSIDE DOWN APPLE TART (TARTE TATIN)

8 medium cooking apples
1 cup sugar, divided
1 teaspoon cinnamon (optional)
½ cup melted butter or margarine
½ recipe flan pastry

1. Heat oven to 400°F.
2. Peel, core and quarter apples. Cut each apple quarter in half. Toss in a bowl with ½ cup sugar and the cinnamon. Turn apples into a 10-inch deep cake pan or shallow casserole.
3. Sprinkle top of apples with remaining sugar and pour melted butter over the top.
4. Roll out dough into a circle to fit top of pan. Place over top of apples. Allow edges of dough to fall inside of pan.
5. Bake about 45 minutes or until apples are tender.
6. Invert tart onto serving dish immediately.
7. Serve warm with whipped cream, if desired.
8. Makes 8 servings.

AMERICAN FRENCH FRUIT TART

1⅔ cups vanilla wafer crumbs
1 tablespoon instant coffee powder
¼ cup butter or margarine, melted
5 egg yolks
¾ cup sugar
3 tablespoons flour
2 cups milk
1 teaspoon vanilla extract
Fresh peaches, pared and sliced
Fresh strawberries, hulled and washed
Fresh blueberries
½ cup red currant jelly

1. Heat oven to 375°F.
2. Combine vanilla crumbs and instant coffee powder. Stir in melted butter and mix well. Pour crumb mixture into a 9-inch pie plate. Press crumbs firmly against bottom and sides, using an 8-inch pie plate.
3. Bake 8 minutes. Cool.
4. Beat egg yolks and sugar together until thick and lemon colored. Slowly beat in flour until well blended.
5. Scald milk with vanilla added. Stir into egg mixture. Return egg mixture to saucepan. Cook over medium heat, stirring constantly, until custard thickens and comes to a boil. Simmer 1 minute.
6. Pour custard into a bowl. Cover the surface of the custard with a circle of waxed paper to prevent a skin forming on top of custard. Cool thoroughly.
7. Spoon custard mixture into pie shell. Top custard with fresh fruit in desired pattern.
8. Melt red currant jelly in a saucepan over low heat. Brush melted jelly over fruit to glaze. Refrigerate until ready to serve.
9. Makes 8 servings.

COUPE AUX MARRONS

18 champagne biscuits or French lady fingers
Vanilla ice cream
Chopped marrons in syrup

1. Arrange 3 champagne biscuits in each individual dessert dish. Place a scoop of vanilla ice cream in each dish. Top with about 1½ tablespoons of marrons in syrup.
2. Makes about 6 servings.

BAVAROIS AUX FRAISES

1 envelope unflavored gelatine
½ cup sugar
Dash of salt
2 eggs, separated
1¼ cups milk
1 pint fresh strawberries, sliced
1 teaspoon vanilla
1 cup heavy cream, whipped

1. Combine gelatine, sugar and salt in a saucepan. Beat together egg yolks and milk. Stir into sugar mixture in saucepan.
2. Place over low heat and cook, stirring constantly, until mixture is thick enough to coat a metal spoon. Cool.
3. Add strawberries and vanilla. Chill until mixture mounds slightly when dropped from a spoon.
4. Beat egg whites until stiff but not dry. Fold in gelatine mixture and whipped cream. Pour into a 1½-quart mold. Chill until firm.
5. Unmold on a serving plate and garnish with strawberries, if desired.
6. Makes 6 servings.

STRAWBERRY SOUR CREAM BISQUE

1 pint fresh strawberries, cleaned and thinly sliced
1 quart dairy sour cream
1 cup sugar
½ cup almond macaroon crumbs
1 teaspoon vanilla
Dash of salt

1. In a bowl combine strawberries, sour cream, sugar, macaroon crumbs, vanilla and salt.
2. Turn mixture into individual molds, small paper cups or refrigerator trays.
3. Place in freezing compartment and freeze until firm.
4. Before serving, remove from freezer and let stand in the refrigerator or at room temperature about 15 or 20 minutes before serving.
5. Makes 8 servings.

CHARLOTTE RUSSE

12 lady fingers
2 envelopes unflavored gelatine
1 cup sugar, divided
¼ teaspoon salt
4 eggs, separated
2½ cups milk
2 tablespoons brandy
1 cup heavy cream, whipped

1. Split lady fingers in halves. Cut a small sliver off one end of each and discard. Stand upright around sides of an 8-inch spring form pan. Set aside.
2. Combine gelatine, ½ cup sugar and salt in a saucepan. Beat together egg yolks and milk. Stir into gelatine mixture. Cook over low heat, stirring constantly, until gelatine is dissolved, about 5 minutes.
3. Remove from heat and add brandy. Chill until mixture mounds slightly when dropped from a spoon.
4. Beat egg whites until stiff but not dry. Gradually add remaining ½ cup sugar and beat until very stiff.
5. Fold gelatine mixture into egg whites. Fold whipped cream into mixture.
6. Carefully pour mixture into prepared pan. Chill in refrigerator until firm.
7. To unmold, release spring and remove sides of mold carefully. Place on a serving plate and garnish with additional whipped cream, if desired.
8. Makes 12 servings.

SHERRY CREAM MOLD

2 envelopes unflavored gelatine
1½ cups milk
¾ cup sugar
¼ teaspoon salt
4 eggs, separated
½ cup sweet sherry
1½ cups heavy cream
Ladyfingers, split in half lengthwise

1. Sprinkle gelatine over top of milk in top part of double boiler. Let stand a few minutes to soften gelatine.
2. Place over water that is just simmering. Stir in sugar, salt and beaten egg yolks. Cook, stirring occasionally, until mixture coats a metal spoon.
3. Remove from heat and blend in sherry. Fill bottom of double boiler with ice water. Place top of double boiler in ice water to hasten chilling.

4. Beat egg whites until they stand in soft peaks. Beat cream until stiff.
5. When egg yolk mixture has thickened slightly, fold mixture into beaten egg whites. Then fold in cream.
6. Lightly butter the sides of a 2-quart mold. Arrange ladyfinger halves around edge of mold. If necessary, trim top edge with sharp knife or scissors until level with top of mold. Turn custard mixture into mold.
7. Chill in refrigerator 3 or 4 hours or overnight.
8. When ready to serve, loosen around sides with a thin bladed knife and invert on a serving plate. Lift off mold.
9. Makes 10 servings.

STRAWBERRY CUSTARD PIE
(shown opposite)

1 package (3¾ ounces) vanilla pudding and pie filling mix
1 baked 10-inch pie shell, cooled
8 ladyfingers, split
1 pint strawberries
1 jar (10 ounces) red currant jelly
2 teaspoons water
Whipped cream or prepared whipped topping

1. Prepare pie filling mix as directed on package. Cool for 5 minutes, stirring twice, to prevent a skin from forming. Pour filling into pie shell. Cool to room temperature.
2. Place ladyfinger halves, cut side down, over top of pie filling. Hull strawberries and cut in half. Arrange berry halves, cut side down, in circles over top of ladyfingers, placing halves close together.
3. Heat jelly with water until softened. Blend until smooth. Cool; then spoon over berries. Chill.
4. Just before serving, border pie with prepared whipped topping or whipped cream.

CAFE BRÛLOT DIABOLIQUE

6 lumps sugar
8 whole cloves
1 stick cinnamon, about 1 inch long
1 lemon peel, cut into strips
4 ounces cognac
4 cups hot, very strong coffee

1. Place all ingredients except coffee in a chafing dish. Do not stir. Ignite cognac with a match and stir carefully until ingredients are well blended.
2. Slowly pour in hot coffee and continue to stir.
3. To serve, ladle into demitasse cups.
4. Makes about 10 demitasse cup servings.

STRAWBERRY BAVARIAN CREAM

   3 envelopes unflavored gelatine
   1 cup cold water
   1 cup sugar
   ¼ teaspoon salt
   2 cups mashed strawberries, juice and pulp
   2 tablespoons lemon juice
   2 cups heavy cream, whipped

1. Sprinkle gelatine on cold water in a 2½-quart saucepan to soften. Place over low heat, cook stirring constantly, until gelatine is dissolved. Remove from heat.

2. Add sugar and salt and stir until sugar is dissolved. Stir in mashed strawberries and lemon juice. Chill until mixture is the consistency of unbeaten egg whites.

3. Fold in heavy whipped cream. Turn mixture into a 2-quart mold. Chill until firm. When ready to serve, unmold on a serving plate. Garnish with fresh strawberries and mint leaves if desired.

4. Makes 8 to 10 servings.

BAVARIAN CREAM

2 envelopes unflavored gelatine
1 cup sugar, divided
¼ teaspoon salt
4 eggs, separated
2½ cups milk
1 teaspoon vanilla
2 cups heavy cream, whipped

1. Combine gelatine, ½ cup sugar and salt in a deep saucepan. Beat together egg yolks and milk. Stir into gelatine mixture. Place saucepan over low heat, cook, stirring constantly, until gelatine is dissolved. This will take about 5 minutes.
2. Remove from heat and add vanilla.
3. Place saucepan in refrigerator and chill until mixture mounds slightly when dropped from a spoon.
4. Beat egg whites until stiff, but not dry. Gradually add remaining ½ cup sugar and beat until very stiff.
5. Lightly place egg whites on top of gelatine mixture. With a rubber scraper, fold egg whites into gelatine mixture. Fold in whipped cream.
6. Turn mixture into a 10-cup mold. Place in refrigerator and chill until firm.
7. Unmold onto a chilled serving plate. Serve plain or with any desired fresh fruit.
8. Makes 8 to 10 servings.

BRANDIED COFFEE JELLY

2 envelopes unflavored gelatine
⅔ cup sugar
4 tablespoons instant coffee powder
¼ teaspoon salt
Water
4 tablespoons brandy

1. Combine gelatine, sugar, instant coffee powder and salt in a saucepan. Add 1 cup water. Place over low heat and cook, stirring constantly, until gelatine and sugar are dissolved. Remove from heat.
2. Add 2½ cups water and brandy. Pour into a 4-cup mold, 8 stemmed glasses or a serving dish. Chill until firm.
3. Unmold and garnish with whipped cream if desired.
4. Makes 8 servings.

COCONUT CREAM WITH STRAWBERRY RUM SAUCE

2 cups light cream, divided
2 envelopes unflavored gelatine
¼ cup cold water
1 cup sugar
2 cups flaked coconut
1½ teaspoons almond extract
3 cups heavy cream, whipped
Strawberry Rum Sauce

1. Put 1½ cups light cream in a saucepan. Bring just to a boil.
2. Sprinkle gelatine over remaining light cream, combined with cold water. Let stand a few minutes to soften.
3. Add softened gelatine and sugar to hot cream. Stir until sugar and gelatine are thoroughly dissolved.
4. Cool to lukewarm. Stir in coconut and almond extract. Fold in whipped cream. Turn mixture into a 2-quart mold. Chill until firm.
5. At serving time, unmold on a platter and serve with Strawberry Rum Sauce.
6. Makes 10 servings.

STRAWBERRY RUM SAUCE

½ cup sugar
2 pints strawberries, cleaned and halved
1⅓ cups water
¼ cup lemon juice
2 tablespoons cornstarch
3 tablespoons light rum

1. Combine sugar and strawberries. Let mixture stand several hours.
2. Drain and reserve syrup.
3. In a saucepan combine ⅔ cup of the strawberry syrup, water, lemon juice and cornstarch. Add strawberries and rum. Bring to a boil slowly, and boil ½ minute.
4. Chill and serve with Coconut Cream.

OEUFS À LA NEIGE

1 quart milk
Sugar
1 teaspoon vanilla
6 eggs, separated
½ teaspoon cornstarch
Salt
2 tablespoons rum or cognac

1. Pour milk into a skillet and bring to a boil over medium heat. Add 6 tablespoons sugar and vanilla. Stir to dissolve sugar.
2. Beat the egg whites until stiff. Gradually beat in 6 tablespoons sugar, cornstarch and a pinch of salt. Beat until mixture stands in stiff peaks.
3. Scoop up egg whites with two large spoons, shaping into egg-shaped ovals. Drop a few at a time into milk mixture, just barely simmering. Cook about 30 seconds on one side, then turn over with a slotted spoon. Cook second side for 30 seconds.
4. Drain egg shapes, which should be firm to the touch, on paper toweling. Repeat cooking until all egg whites are used.
5. Beat egg yolks until light and lemon colored. Gradually add some of the hot milk, stirring constantly. Pour beaten eggs and remaining milk mixture into a heavy saucepan. Cook over low heat, stirring constantly, until custard coats a metal spoon.
6. Remove from heat and stir in rum or cognac. Strain custard mixture into a wide shallow serving dish. Cover top of custard with egg shapes. Chill.
7. Put ½ cup sugar in a small heavy skillet. Cook over low heat, stirring constantly, until sugar melts and becomes light brown in color. Do not let the mixture burn.
8. Immediately pour the hot caramel syrup over the top of the egg whites. Chill.
9. Makes about 10 servings.

VANILLA MOUSSE WITH STRAWBERRY SAUCE
(shown opposite)

1½ cups milk
1½ cup sugar, divided
2 eggs, separated
2 envelopes unflavored gelatine
Water
1 tablespoon vanilla
1 pint heavy cream, whipped
1 pint fresh strawberries
1 tablespoon cornstarch
½ cup lemon juice
2 tablespoons butter

1. Combine milk and 1 cup sugar in top of double boiler. Place over low heat and heat just until bubbles form around edge of milk.
2. Beat egg yolks in a bowl. Gradually stir in hot milk. Return mixture to double boiler. Cook over hot water, stirring occasionally, until mixture coats a metal spoon.
3. Soften gelatine in ½ cup water.
4. Remove custard from heat. Stir in softened gelatine and continue stirring until gelatine is dissolved. Stir in vanilla.
5. Fill bottom of double boiler with ice water. Place top part in the ice water. Cool until custard mounds when dropped from a spoon. Beat with a rotary beater until light and frothy.
6. Beat egg whites until stiff but not dry. Fold into custard mixture.
7. Fold cream into custard mixture. Turn mixture into a 2-quart mold. Chill until set.
8. Clean and hull berries. Reserve 1 cup of the best berries for garnish. Force the remaining through a food mill or blend in an electric blender. Put through a strainer to remove seeds.
9. Combine the remaining ½ cup sugar with cornstarch in a medium saucepan. Gradually stir in 1 cup water.
10. Cook over medium heat, stirring, until sauce thickens and boils for ½ minute.
11. Remove from heat and stir in lemon juice, butter and puréed strawberries. Chill sauce.
12. To serve, unmold mousse onto a serving platter. Garnish with whole strawberries. Pipe a row of whipped cream around bottom of mold, if desired. Serve with cooked, chilled strawberry sauce.
13. Makes 8 to 10 servings.

California Strawberry Advisory Board

STRAWBERRY SOUFFLÉ

1 pint fresh strawberries
1¼ cup sugar, divided
1 envelope unflavored gelatine
4 eggs, separated
⅛ teaspoon salt
1 cup heavy cream, whipped
Brandied Strawberry Sauce

1. Fold a long strip of waxed paper or aluminum foil so that it is about 4 inches wide and long enough to extend around the outside of a 1½-quart soufflé dish. Lightly brush one side of the strip with oil. Fasten the strip, oiled side in, around top of soufflé dish. It can be tied with string or clipped together with paper clips.
2. Clean and crush strawberries. Force berries though a food mill or sieve. There should be about 1⅓ cups purée. Stir ½ cup sugar into the purée.
3. Remove ¼ cup sweetened purée. Sprinkle gelatine over top and let it stand to soften.
4. Combine egg yolks with ½ cup sugar in top of double boiler. Cook over boiling water, stirring, until mixture is thickened. Add gelatine mixture and stir until gelatine is dissolved.
5. Remove from hot water and cool. Blend in remaining strawberry purée.
6. Beat egg whites and salt until foamy. Gradually add remaining ¼ cup sugar and contine beating until mixture is shiny and holds stiff peaks. Fold in whipped cream. Gently fold in strawberry mixture.
7. Turn mixture into prepared soufflé dish. Chill until firm.
8. Remove collar and serve with Brandied Strawberry Sauce.
9. Makes 6 servings.

Cold Strawberry Soufflé is picture pretty, high and handsome in its serving dish. Served with Brandied Strawberry Sauce, every bite is truly heavenly!

California Strawberry Advisory Board

BRANDIED STRAWBERRY SAUCE

1 pint fresh strawberries
1 cup sugar
2 tablespoons cornstarch
2 tablespoons lemon juice
2 tablespoons cognac

1. Clean and crush strawberries.
2. In a saucepan combine sugar and cornstarch. Stir in lemon juice and crushed strawberries. Cook over medium heat, stirring, until sauce is thickened and clear.
3. Cool slightly. Stir in cognac. Chill well before serving with Strawberry Soufflé.
4. Makes about 1½ cups sauce.

SOUFFLÉ AUX MARRONS

2 tablespoons butter
2 tablespoons flour
1 cup milk
1 cup chestnut puree, unsweetened
½ cup sugar
2 squares unsweetened chocolate, melted
4 eggs, separated
1 teaspoon vanilla

1. Heat oven to 375°F.
2. Butter heavily the bottom and sides of a 1½-quart soufflé dish. Sprinkle butter-coated surface with granulated sugar. Shake out excess sugar.
3. Melt butter in a saucepan. Stir in flour. Remove from heat.
4. Put milk, chestnut purée and sugar in a bowl and beat with a rotary beater until smooth and well blended. Gradually stir chestnut mixture into the flour mixture.
5. Cook over low heat, stirring constantly, until thickened. Stir melted chocolate into chestnut mixture and remove from heat.
6. Beat egg yolks. Gradually stir hot chestnut sauce into egg yolks and stir until smooth. Cool.
7. Beat egg whites until stiff but not dry. Fold egg whites and vanilla into chestnut mixture. Pour mixture into prepared soufflé dish.
8. Place soufflé dish in a pan and add hot water to ½-inch depth in pan. Bake 40 to 45 minutes or until soufflé has risen and is set.
9. Serve immediately.
10. Makes 6 to 8 servings.

VANILLA SOUFFLÉ

3 tablespoons butter
3 tablespoons flour
¾ cup warm milk
¼ cup sugar
  Pinch of salt
4 egg yolks, well beaten
1 teaspoon vanilla
5 egg whites, stiffly beaten

1. Heat oven to 375°F.
2. Melt butter in a saucepan. Remove from heat and stir in flour. Return to heat and cook over low heat 1 minute. Remove from heat.
3. Add milk gradually and stir until smooth. Stir in sugar and salt.
4. Cook over low heat, stirring constantly, until mixture comes to a boil and is smooth and thickened. Remove from heat and stir quickly into beaten egg yolks. Stir until well blended. Stir in vanilla.
5. Add half the beaten egg whites to the custard mixture and fold in lightly but thoroughly. Be sure the mixture is blended evenly. Do not stir, as this will lose the air incorporated in the egg whites and the soufflé will not rise.
6. Add remaining egg whites and fold in quickly. A few patches of egg whites in the mixture will not matter, if the first incorporation has been complete.
7. Butter a 1½-quart straight-sided soufflé dish. Dust with sugar, until it is well coated. Shake out excess sugar.
8. Turn mixture into prepared soufflé dish. Bake 25 to 28 minutes. Remove from oven and serve immediately with whipped cream or sauce, if desired. It is also excellent served alone with no sauce.
9. Makes 4 servings. (It will make 6 servings, but not if every one loves soufflé.)

Variations

Almond Soufflé: Substitute almond extract for the vanilla extract. Stir in ½ cup blanched, grated almonds before folding in the egg whites.

Coffee Soufflé: Use half very strong coffee and half milk in place of all milk.

Lemon Soufflé: Omit the vanilla. Stir in the juice and grated rind of 1 lemon before folding in the egg whites.

Liqueur Soufflé: Omit the vanilla. Stir in ¼ cup Grand Marnier, Benedictine, Cointreau or Maraschino before folding in the egg whites.

Nut Soufflé: Stir 1 cup finely chopped nuts into custard mixture before folding in the egg whites.

SOUFFLÉ GLACÉ À L'ORANGE

⅔ cup crumbled macaroons
6 tablespoons Cointreau, divided
3 eggs
  Sugar
⅛ teaspoon salt
2 tablespoons dry white wine
1 tablespoon chopped marrons, in syrup
2 teaspoons toasted ground filberts
3 cups heavy cream
¼ cup sifted confectioners' sugar
10 orange shells (see note)
4 egg whites
¼ teaspoon cream of tartar
  Sauce Bernadotte

1. Soak crumbled macaroons in 4 tablespoons Cointreau. Set aside.
2. Beat eggs in top of double boiler until very light. Gradually beat in ⅓ cup sugar, salt and dry white wine. Cook over hot, not boiling water, beating with a wire whisk until very fluffy and thick, about 5 to 6 minutes. Immediately turn into a large bowl and continue beating with the whisk until cold.
3. Gently fold in macaroon mixture, marrons and ground filberts. Beat cream just until stiff and fold into cooked custard. Sift confectioners' sugar over top and fold in. Carefully add remaining Cointreau.
4. Spoon mixture into orange shells. Place in freezer and freeze until firm. If you are going to use these at a much later time, they should be wrapped in moisture-vapor proof wrapping.
5. Heat oven to 475°F.
6. Beat egg whites until frothy; add cream of tartar and beat to soft peaks. Gradually beat in ½ cup sugar. Continue beating until egg whites are very stiff but not dry. Remove orange shells from freezer. Spread meringue quickly all over top of filling. Place on a baking pan and bake 2 to 3 minutes or until meringue is lightly browned.
7. Serve immediately with Sauce Bernadotte.
8. Makes 10 servings.

Note: To make orange cups, wash large navel oranges. Cut ¼ to ⅓ from top of each orange. Carefully ream juice from oranges, keeping shells intact. Remove pulp from inside shells with a small spoon, being careful not to pierce skin. Scallops edges of orange cups if desired. Refrigerate before filling.

SAUCE BERNADOTTE

½ cup sugar
1 tablespoon cornstarch
Pinch of salt
2 cups orange juice
1 tablespoon butter
2 teaspoons grated orange peel
2 egg yolks, beaten
½ cup finely chopped fresh orange sections, well drained (from orange cups)
1 cup heavy cream, whipped
¼ cup Grand Marnier

1. Combine sugar, cornstarch and salt in a saucepan. Blend in orange juice. Add butter. Bring to a boil over medium heat, stirring constantly, and boil 1 minute. Add grated orange peel.
2. Blend some of the hot mixture into the beaten egg yolks. Return mixture to saucepan. Cook over low heat 1 minute.
3. Fold in orange sections. Turn into a bowl and chill until cold.
4. Fold in whipped cream and Grand Marnier. Serve chilled with Soufflé Glacé a l'Orange.
5. Makes 3¾ cups sauce.

OMELET SOUFFLÉ

8 eggs, separated
½ cup sugar
⅓ cup cognac or rum

1. Heat oven to 375°F.
2. Beat egg yolks until light and lemon-colored. Gradually beat in sugar. Stir in Cognac.
3. Beat egg whites until they stand in stiff peaks. Fold ⅓ of the egg whites into yolk mixture until they are well blended. Fold in remaining egg whites gently without losing too much air.
4. Heat a heavy metal skillet with an oven proof handle. Use a 10-inch aluminum omelet skillet if you have one. When skillet is hot, butter it well and sprinkle with granulated sugar. Pour soufflé mixture into skillet.
5. Bake 15 minutes. Remove from oven, sprinkle with granulated sugar and serve at once.
6. If desired, sprinkle with 2 tablespoons warm Cognac and ignite with a match before serving.
7. Makes about 6 servings.

CRÈME BRÛLÉE

6 eggs
⅔ cup sugar
½ teaspoon salt
2 cups milk
2 cups heavy cream
1 teaspoon vanilla
¾ cup firmly packed light brown sugar

1. Heat oven to 350°F.
2. Beat eggs slightly. Beat in sugar and salt. Add milk and cream gradually, stirring constantly. Add vanilla.
3. Pour mixture into a shallow 1½-quart baking dish. Place casserole in a shallow pan of hot water.
4. Bake about 60 minutes or until a knife inserted in the center comes out clean.
5. Cool. Chill custard in refrigerator.
6. Preheat broiling compartment with racks removed.
7. Carefully sift brown sugar over top of custard to about ¼-inch thickness, leaving center uncovered, if desired.
8. Set custard on broiler rack about 3 inches from source of heat. Broil about 4 minutes, or until sugar carmelizes and forms a crust. Watch carefully because the sugar burns very quickly.
9. Chill in refrigerator before serving.
10. Makes 10 servings.

Note: This can be baked in 6 individual serving dishes. In which case, use only 4 eggs and bake 35 to 40 minutes, or until a knife inserted in the center comes out clean.

MOCK CRÈME BRÛLÉE

2 packages (3½ ounces each) vanilla pudding and pie filling mix
3 cups milk
1 cup cream
½ cup brown sugar, firmly packed
½ cup chopped pecans

1. Cook pudding as directed on package using 3 cups milk and 1 cup cream. Cool slightly.
2. Pour pudding into a shallow 1½-quart baking dish. Chill thoroughly.
3. Preheat broiler compartment without rack. Sprinkle brown sugar evenly over surface of pudding. Sprinkle pecans over top of sugar. Place pudding on broiler rack, 5 inches from source of heat, and broil 4 to 5 minutes or until brown sugar melts and becomes bubbly. Watch carefully so that it does not burn.
4. Makes 8 servings.

POTS DE LA CRÈME AU CHOCOLAT

3 squares unsweetened chocolate
3 cups milk
⅔ cup sugar
¼ teaspoon salt
5 egg yolks, beaten
½ teaspoon vanilla
   Heavy cream

1. Cut chocolate squares into small pieces, or shave it into curls with a vegetable peeler. Combine with milk in a saucepan. Cook over very low heat, stirring, until chocolate has melted. Add sugar and salt and continue cooking until mixture is smooth.
2. Remove from heat and slowly stir into beaten egg yolks. Return mixture to saucepan and cook over very low heat, stirring constantly, until mixture thickens.
3. Remove from heat and stir in vanilla. Pour into custard cups or covered French china pots. Chill.
4. Serve with thick, heavy cream.
5. Makes 6 servings.

CARAMEL TOPPED EGG NOG CUSTARD

½ cup sugar
2½ cups canned egg nog
2 eggs
¼ teaspoon salt
2 tablespoons rum, optional

1. Heat oven to 325°F.
2. In a small heavy skillet, heat sugar over low heat until it melts and turns into a light, golden brown syrup. Stir constantly while sugar is melting. Pour about 1 tablespoonful of the hot syrup into five 5-ounce custard cups. Let cool.
3. In a medium-sized saucepan, scald egg nog.
4. Beat eggs with salt. Slowly stir hot egg nog into beaten eggs. Stir in rum, if desired. Pour mixture over syrup in custard cups. Set cups in a baking pan. Pour warm water into pan to depth of 1 inch.
5. Bake 1 hour and 30 minutes or until a knife inserted ½ inch from edge of custard cup comes out clean. Remove from oven and remove cups from hot water. Let cool at room temperature.
6. Chill in refrigerator about 2 hours or until

well chilled. At serving time, carefully insert a knife around side of cup to loosen custard; invert cups over dessert dishes and quickly turn out custards and caramel syrup.
7. Makes 5 servings.

PEARS HÉLÈNE
(shown opposite)

6 small fresh pears
2 cups sugar, divided
   Water
1 teaspoon vanilla
½ cup light corn syrup
   Dash of salt
2 squares (2 ounces) semi-sweet chocolate
½ cup light cream
1 tablespoon butter
1 quart vanilla ice cream

1. Peel pears. Cut in half lengthwise and core. Combine 1½ cups sugar, 1½ cups water and vanilla in a large saucepan. Bring to a boil, stirring until sugar is dissolved.
2. Add pear halves to sugar mixture and simmer gently about 8 minutes, or just until pears are tender. Transfer fruit and juice to a dish and chill in the refrigerator.
3. Combine corn syrup, remaining sugar, 2 tablespoons water and salt in a saucepan. Bring to a boil and stir until sugar is dissolved. Bring to a full rolling boil and boil 3 minutes. Remove from heat. Add chocolate and stir until melted. Stir in cream and butter. Beat with rotary beater until smooth.
4. To serve, drain pears and arrange 2 halves in each dessert dish. Cover with a large serving of ice cream. Pour warm or chilled chocolate syrup over the top, as desired.
5. Makes 6 servings.

CHAMPAGNE FRUIT CUP

1 can (11 ounces) mandarin orange sections, chilled
1 can (1 pound) Queen Anne cherries, pitted and chilled
1 cup halved, seeded grapes
1 cup diced, unpeeled red apple
Chilled champagne

1. Drain mandarin orange sections and cherries. Combine with grapes and apples. Chill.
2. At serving time spoon into saucer shaped champagne or sherbert glasses. Fill glasses with chilled champagne.
3. Makes 8 to 10 servings.

FRAISES À LA CRÈME AU PETIT-LAIT
(STRAWBERRIES WITH FRENCH BUTTERMILK CREAM)

1 quart buttermilk
1 pint heavy cream
1¼ cups sugar
1 teaspoon vanilla
2 pints fresh strawberries
¼ cup confectioners' sugar

1. Blend together buttermilk, cream, sugar and vanilla. Pour into freezing trays and freeze until firm.
2. Clean strawberries and cut in half. Sprinkle with confectioners' sugar and chill 15 minutes.
3. Beat the frozen buttermilk cream until smooth. Serve with chilled strawberries.
4. Makes 6 servings.

SHERRY BAKED PEARS

½ cup sherry
½ cup water
½ cup brown sugar
2 tablespoons fresh lemon juice
3 tablespoons butter or margarine
4 fresh pears

1. Heat oven to 350°F.
2. Combine sherry, water, sugar, lemon juice and butter in a small saucepan. Simmer over medium heat about 5 minutes.
3. While sauce is cooking, halve, pare and core pears. Arrange pears in a baking dish. Pour sherry sauce over pears. Cover dish.
4. Bake about 35 to 40 minutes or until pears are tender.
5. Serve warm or chilled, plain or with whipped or sour cream, if desired.
6. Makes 4 servings.

STRAWBERRIES AND CHAMPAGNE

4 pints fresh strawberries
⅔ cup sugar
½ cup cognac
Chilled champagne

1. Clean and hull strawberries. Sprinkle with sugar and cognac. Cover and chill several hours.
2. Spoon strawberries into dessert glasses. Pour champagne over berries.
3. Makes 8 servings.

Note: Champagne is also excellent with other fresh fruits such as raspberries or sliced fresh peaches.

VINTAGE BAKED APPLES

6 baking apples
¼ cup brown sugar, firmly packed
¾ cup port
6 whole cloves
1 stick cinnamon, about 3 inches
1 tablespoon lemon juice

1. Heat oven to 375°F.
2. Core apples and pare down about ¼ way from stem. Place apples in a baking dish.
3. Combine remaining ingredients in a saucepan. Bring to a boil and simmer about 5 minutes. Pour sauce over apples.
4. Bake about 45 minutes or until apples are tender. Baste occasionally with sauce in bottom of baking dish.
5. Serve warm or chilled, plain or with cream.
6. Makes 6 servings.

ORANGE ORIENTAL

3 large oranges
2 cups sugar
1 cup water
Candied violets (optional)

1. With a vegetable peeler remove just the outer orange rind from the oranges. Cut rind in slivers and place in a saucepan with sugar and water. Place over medium heat and simmer until slivers are tender.
2. Peel oranges until all of the white part of the rind is removed. Cut oranges in half crosswise. Place in a serving dish.
3. Pour hot sugar syrup over oranges. Refrigerate until thoroughly chilled.
4. Garnish with candied violets before servings, if desired.
5. Makes 6 servings.

WINE-BUTTER GLAZED PEACHES

    3 tablespoons butter
    2 tablespoons lemon juice
    6 small ripe peaches, peeled
    ⅓ cup brown sugar
    ⅓ cup rosé wine
    ½ cup heavy cream

1. Melt butter in a large skillet over medium heat. Add lemon juice and peaches. Turn peaches over and over to coat with butter.
2. Sprinkle with brown sugar and add wine to pan.
3. Poach over low heat, turning often, about 15 minutes or until peaches are heated through and lightly glazed.
4. Push peaches to one side and stir in cream. Bring just to the boil. Lower heat and simmer several minutes.
5. Serve peaches warm with some of the wine-cream sauce.
6. Makes 6 servings.

Glossary of Terms

AU GRATIN: Gratin is the brown coating on food formed by broiling or baking in the oven. Au gratin has come to mean a method of preparing food in a sauce whose surface is covered with butter, bread crumbs or grated cheese and baked or broiled until lightly browned.

BATTER: A mixture of flour, liquid, and other ingredients, used as a basis for cakes, fritters, coating or pancakes. Its consistency may range from a thin liquid to a stiff, thick one, depending on the proportions of the ingredients.

BASTE: To moisten food while it is cooking, by spooning on melted fat, pan juices, wine or any other liquid.

BEAT: To mix ingredients together making a smooth batter, using a wire whisk, spoon, electric mixer or rotary beater.

BEATING EGG WHITES: To incorporate as much air as possible into the egg whites as you beat, thus increasing their volume. They can be beaten with a wire whisk, electric mixer or rotary beater.

BEATING EGG WHITES STIFF: Egg whites should stand in peaks, drooping over a bit. Surface should still be moist and glossy.

BEATING EGG WHITES VERY STIFF: Egg whites should stand in upright peaks, without drooping. Surface of egg whites should be dry.

BLANCH: To plunge food into boiling water for the purpose of removing skins, as with almonds, or for partial precooking as when freezing foods.

BLEND: To combine two or more ingredients well, usually with a spoon or electric mixer.

BOIL: To cook food in a boiling liquid in which bubbles constantly rise to the surface and break. In a rapid boil, the bubbles are vigorous and rolling. In a medium boil, the bubbles are gentle. In a very slow boil, the liquid hardly moves and is called a simmer.

BONE: To remove bones from meat or fowl as directed in some recipes.

BOUQUET GARNI: A combination of parsley, thyme and bay leaf for flavoring soups, stews, sauces and braised meat dishes. If the herbs are fresh and in sprigs, the parsley is folded around them and they are tied together. If the herbs are dried, they are wrapped in a piece of cheesecloth and tied. The bundle is made so that the herbs can be removed easily before serving.

BRAISE: To brown well in a little hot fat, then adding a small amount of liquid and cooking in a tightly covered pan over very low heat until tender.

BREAD: To coat food with dry bread crumbs or cracker crumbs. The food is often dipped first into a liquid or a beaten egg to help the crumbs stick to the surface.

BROTH: The liquid in which meat, fish, poultry or vegetables, or a combination of them, have been cooked.

BROWN: To turn the surface of food brown in color by cooking in hot fat on top of the range or at high temperature in the oven or broiler.

BRUSH ON: To apply melted fat, salad oil, cream, beaten egg, etc. to the surface of food with a pastry brush or crumpled waxed paper.

CARAMELIZE: To melt granulated sugar in a large skillet over medium heat, stirring constantly until sugar turns into a golden nut brown syrup. This is used either to line a dessert mold or to add flavor or color to other mixtures.

CEPES: Members of the mushroom family, apparently native to France. They sometimes grow exceedingly large and have a most unusual texture and flavor. In America, they can be found canned and packed in brine or deep fat fried. They may be used for an hors d'oeuvre, entrée or vegetable course.

CHILL: To place in the refrigerator or over cracked ice until cold.

CHOP: To cut food into small pieces. Place food to be chopped on a wooden board, hold tip of a French knife close to the surface of the board with one hand, then move knife handle vigorously up and down on the food with the other hand. Repeat several times, until food is thoroughly chopped.

CLARIFY: To clear a liquid, such as soup, by adding slightly beaten egg white (and the egg shells, if desired). These coagulate the particles in the liquid, which are then strained out.

COAT A METAL SPOON: A term that describes the degree of thickness of a sauce or custard. To test, stir liquid with a metal spoon, hold spoon above the pan and allow it to drip. It should retain an even film or coating of the liquid. A spoon dipped into a custard should emerge with a fairly thick coating.

CODDLE: To cook slowly in a liquid heated to just below the boiling point.

COMBINE: To mix or blend together two or more ingredients.

CONDIMENT: Any seasoning added to food to enhance its flavor.

COOL: To let stand at room temperature until cool to the touch.

CREAM: To rub or work fat such as butter or margarine with sugar against the sides of a bowl until light and creamy. Or to use an electric mixer until mixture is soft and creamy.

CRISP: To make firm. Leafy vegetables such as lettuce are rinsed in water and chilled. Dry foods, such as bread and crackers, are heated in an oven at a very low temperature.

CROUTONS: Bread cut into ½-inch cubes, tossed in a little melted butter or margarine (with a bit of garlic if desired), then broiled or toasted in a 300° F. oven. Served as a garnish in soups or salads.

CRUMB: To break into small pieces. Fresh bread crumbs are made by pulling a piece of fresh bread into small, soft particles. Stale bread crumbs are made with dried out bread by crushing with a rolling pin or in a blender. Refrigerate stale crumbs and use to coat croquettes and other foods.

CRUSH: To pulverize by rolling with a rolling pin until consistency of coarse powder. Fruits are usually crushed by mashing until they lose their shape.

CUBE: To cut into small equal-sized pieces ¼- to ½-inch square.

CUT IN: To combine solid fat with flour in pastry making. Using two knives, scissor fashion, or a pastry blender, cut shortening into flour or flour mixture until flour-coated fat particles are of desired size.

DEGLAZE: To use browned bits in pan for au jus sauce. After meat has been roasted or browned in a skillet on top of the stove, all of the grease should be poured off. Liquid is then added to the pan and as it simmers, browned bits from the bottom are stirred up and incorporated with the sauce.

DEGREASE: To remove fat from a liquid. Let the liquid stand for a few minutes so that the fat will rise to the top. Tip the container slightly and skim the fat from the surface with a spoon. Wrap an ice cube in a piece of paper toweling, draw it over the surface to soak up any remaining fat. If time permits, refrigerate the liquid in its container until the fat congeals on the surface, thus making it simple to lift off.

DEVEIN: To remove the black or white vein running along the back of a shrimp. With a sharp knife, make a shallow cut along the vein line, then lift or scrape out the vein.

DICE: To cut into very small even cubes.

DISSOLVE: To mix a dry substance with a liquid until it dissolves; or to heat it until it melts.

DOT: To scatter small bits of butter or margarine over the surface of food.

DRAIN: To remove liquid by pouring food into a colander or strainer until the liquid has dripped out, or by tipping pan while holding lid in place so that just the liquid is poured off.

DREDGE: To coat food with flour, sugar, bread or cracker crumbs.

DUST: To sprinkle food lightly with sugar, flour or crumbs.

ESCALOPE: A thin slice of meat, usually veal, that has been flattened.

FILET: To remove flesh of fish, poultry or meat from the bone prior to cooking. A filet is thus a piece of fish, poultry or meat without bone. The term also refers to the tenderloin of beef. A filet mignon is a steak cut from the smaller end of a filet of beef.

FLAKE: To break into small pieces with a fork, as in cooked fish recipes.

FLAMBÉ: A French term meaning blazing.

FOIE GRAS: The liver of a goose or duck fattened in a special way. Some of the best ones in France weigh as much as four pounds apiece. Pure foie gras is packed in tins and is usually sold only to restaurants because it is quite expensive. Mixtures of foie gras with other kinds of livers and seasonings, sold as pâté de foie gras, are available in many supermarkets and are excellent.

FOLD: To incorporate a delicate mixture into a thicker, heavier one, as folding in beaten egg whites or whipped cream. Place egg whites or cream on top of heavier mixture. Pass a rubber spatula down through mixture and across bottom of pan or bowl, bring up some of the mixture and place on top of egg whites or cream. Repeat until egg whites or cream are evenly combined with mixture. This should be done quickly but gently.

FRY: To cook in a very small amount of hot fat.

GRATE: To rub food on a grater to produce fine, medium or coarse particles. When grating lemon or orange rind, grate only the colored part of the rind.

GREASE: To rub the surface of food or utensils lightly with butter, margarine, shortening or salad oil.

GRIND: To cut food into small particles with a food grinder.

JULIENNE: To cut food into thin, match-like strips.

KNEAD: To work dough by pressing it with the heels of the hands, folding, turning and pressing; usually applied to yeast dough and worked on a floured board. Yeast dough should be kneaded

until it looks full and rounded, smooth, satiny and tightly stretched.

LARD: To insert small pieces of fat in lean meat for flavor or juiciness. Fat may be put in gashes in the meat or run through with a larding needle. Pieces of fat salt pork or bacon placed over meat may be substituted for larding. This prevents meat from drying out and bastes it while cooking.

MARINATE: To let food stand in a seasoned liquid to enhance its flavor or make it more tender.

MARROW: The fatty filling of beef leg-bones. This is considered a delicacy in many types of cookery. It is poached and used in sauces, garnitures and on crisp toast as canapés.

MASH: To soften and break down by using a masher, the back of a spoon, a fork, or by forcing through a sieve.

MELT: To change fat into a liquid state by heating.

MINCE: To cut or chop very fine, with a chopper or a French knife.

MOUND: A spoonful of a mixture dropped into another mixture. A mound forms a definite heap and does not blend into the original mixture.

PARBOIL: To boil in water or other liquid until partially cooked, preliminary to another form of cooking.

PARE: To remove the outer covering of fruit or vegetables with a knife or paring tool.

PEEL: To pull off the outer covering, as of bananas or oranges.

POACH: To cook food immersed in a liquid that is barely simmering.

PREHEAT: To heat an oven or broiler to a desired temperature before putting in food.

PUREE: To make solid foods into a mush. This may be done with a meat grinder, food mill, an electric blender, or by pushing through a sieve.

REDUCE: To boil down a liquid, reducing it in quantity and concentrating its taste. This is usually done when making a sauce and is a very important step.

ROUX: A mixture of fat and flour blended together over low heat—the first step in making all sauces in which flour is the thickening agent.

SAUTÉ: To fry lightly in a small amount of hot fat.

SCALD: To heat a liquid to just under the boiling point or to the point tiny bubbles appear around the edge of the saucepan. Also, to pour boiling water over food.

SCORE: To make shallow slits or gashes with a knife or fork on the surface of food.

SEAR: To brown the surface of food quickly, over high heat, as in a hot skillet.

SEASON: To add seasonings to one's own taste.

SEPARATE: To separate egg yolks from the whites.

SET: A condition in which liquids have congealed and retain their shape, usually referring to gelatin mixtures.

SHALLOTS: Delicately flavored members of the onion family, having the slightest hint of garlic. They are sold by the pound and keep fairly well. If you do not have shallots, the minced white part of green onions can be substituted very nicely.

SHRED: To cut or break in thin pieces.

SIFT: To put through a flour sifter or fine sieve.

SIMMER: To cook in a liquid at a temperature slightly below boiling.

SKEWER: To hold in place by means of metal or wooden skewers or toothpicks.

SKIM: To remove a substance, usually fat, from the surface of a liquid.

SLIVER: To cut or split into long thin pieces.

SNIP: To cut into small pieces with kitchen shears.

STEEP: To let stand in a hot liquid.

STEW: A thick combination of a variety of foods cooked in liquid at a low temperature for a long period of time.

STIR: To blend with a spoon in a circular motion, widening circles until all ingredients are well mixed.

STOCK: A liquid in which meat, poultry, fish, bones, vegetables and seasonings have been cooked for a long time.

THICKEN: To make a liquid more dense by adding flour, cornstarch or egg yolks.

TOSS: To mix lightly with two forks or a fork and spoon.

TRUFFLES: Called the "black diamonds of gastronomy". They are members of the fungus family and grow underground in one part of France, near a certain type of oak tree. They are usually hunted with the aid of a pig or dog. They are black, roughly shaped, somewhat crisp and have a most luxurious aroma. Truffles from Perigord, traditionally associated with classic French cookery, can be used in many ways and add distinction to many dishes. In America, they are available canned, whole, sliced or just the peelings.

TRUSS: To bind the wings and legs of a fowl before cooking.

UNMOLD: To remove from a mold. Dip a small pointed knife in warm water and run it around inner edges of mold. Dip mold just to rim in warm water for two to three seconds. Remove and shake gently to loosen gelatin. Cover top of mold with chilled, inverted serving plate. Turn plate and mold over together. Lift off mold carefully. If the contents stick, rub the mold gently with a hot, damp towel.

WHIP: To beat rapidly, usually with an electric mixer or rotary beater to incorporate air and increase volume.

INDEX